PETER PENNOYER
ARCHITECTS

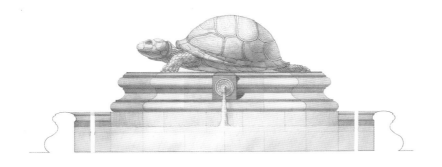

PETER PENNOYER ARCHITECTS
CITY | COUNTRY

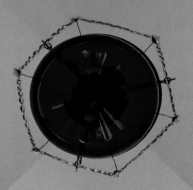

ANNE WALKER
PHOTOGRAPHY BY ERIC PIASECKI

VENDOME
NEW YORK • LONDON

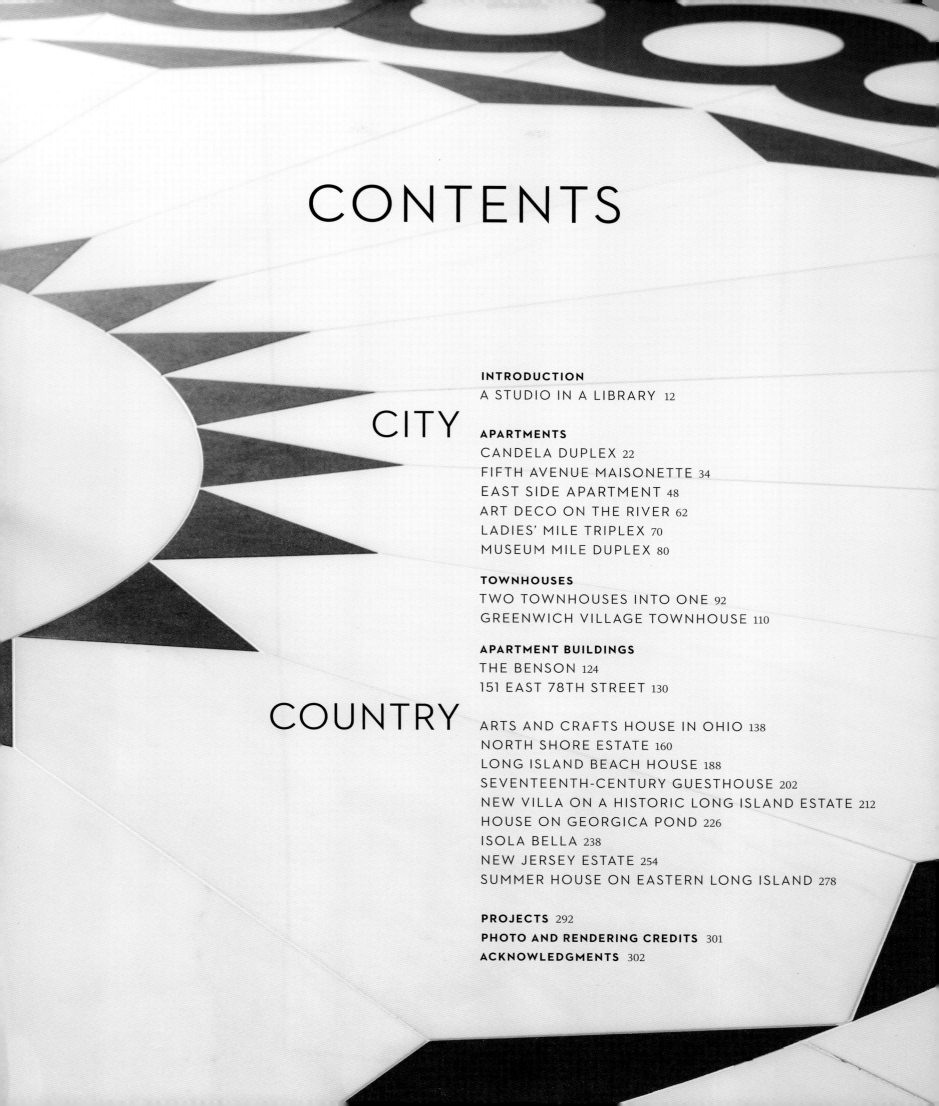

CONTENTS

PETER PENNOYER ARCHITECTS

A STUDIO IN A LIBRARY

At PPA, our library, a long room at the center of our office, is the core of our firm, the wellspring of inspiration for architecture, design, scholarship, and advocacy. Our partner Gregory Gilmartin buys books continually—from dealers, university presses, and more obscure sources. His new acquisitions are arrayed on a round table that we all pass daily, then shelved among thousands of other volumes, all carefully organized according to Gregory's system. This extensive collection is constantly turned to for quick consultations and deeper study. A designer may wonder how a gate might be set into a garden wall or how to resolve the final volute of the railing on a curved stair. A patient search yields illustrations of a variety of historical models. Rather than settle on a single image or approach, we understand that admired architects have solved the same design problem differently. What we cull from these various sources is an interpretation of the wisdom offered by tradition. The books serve not as a crutch but as a spur to our imaginations—imaginations that are continually enriched by looking outside of our world.

Our study of historical precedents becomes internalized once we harness it for a design. Each project builds fluency, and—as with language—fluency is proliferative. It can yield original ideas and reify those once lost to history. Between our print archives and built reality lies the question: what will endure? This exacting inquiry is the philosophical fulcrum of our work at PPA, straddling aesthetics and profession. To practice architecture inspired by classical and traditional sources in the twenty-first century, I believe, bears the precondition that truly enduring design is neither a prescriptive quality nor a replicated form; it is not a fait accompli. Today, however, traditional architecture is often experienced more as an echo than as an art, overwhelmingly expressed through an uncritical

PRECEDING PAGES
The core of PPA's practice
is the library, which contains
more than 10,000 books.

OPPOSITE
PPA's twelve-foot-tall clock
was inspired by the machined
angles found in designs from
the golden age of railroad
travel for the new Moynihan
Train Hall, a space reimagined
by Skidmore, Owings &
Merrill within McKim, Mead
& White's James A. Farley
Post Office Building.

vocabulary of fixed historical elements, rearranged and reconstituted. In our studio, we eschew potted history; instead, we passionately scrutinize our sources and ideas to shape architecture that lasts. We hold classical design to a hypercritical standard: every ornate detail, every flourish, must be studied and justified; historical sources must be fluently resolved within the contemporary context. The pursuit not only of inherent beauty but of a sui generis communion with the present, a sense of belonging: that is what is meaningful, that is what endures.

The question I ask now, writing the introduction to our second monograph, is the same. Looking back at a decade of appreciable artistic growth and professional transformation, what about PPA has endured? In 2010, when we published our first monograph, we were a thirty-person firm specializing primarily in classical and traditional residential work. Since then, we have grown into a broader practice with an Interior Design department, a branch office in South Florida, and projects as far off as Dalian, China, and Hong Kong. Our commissions have expanded to include apartment buildings, museum exhibits, theaters, and projects for the city, including a clock at the center of the Moynihan Train Hall. New leadership has emerged as well, with Jennifer Gerakaris, Tim Kelly, and Gregory Gilmartin joining Tom Nugent and myself as firm principals. History, scholarship, and drawing continue to be central to our practice, but digital programs, software, virtual reality, and 3D printing now rule the profession. Instead of remaining comfortable with the skills that we had mastered, we decided to continue to adopt new digital tools. Having a foot on both sides of this practical crevasse has been both unnerving and rewarding. In this sense, a collaborative enterprise of architects like ours—one that spans more than three decades—becomes stronger; this is how we try to do better work each year.

The library also reminds us of buildings we have seen and all but forgotten. Our most unorthodox project in the past decade is a new house set in an extensive sculpture park. In 2014, the client, Scott Mueller, raised the ante by asking that the design of the house, which had initially been inspired by Arts and Crafts architecture, reflect the influences of Czech Cubism, an obscure style that thrived in and around Prague for just six years before World War I. Czech Cubism was an architecture of oblique angles and crystalline forms that expressed the inner forces of massing rather than the classical arrangement of post and beam. This was foreign to our way of thinking, and I was stumped, but Gregory Gilmartin reminded me that his collection included books on the style that he had acquired when we visited Prague in 1985. Delving into the literature, studying the plans, and finding new publications on the subject, Gilmartin was able to understand Czech Cubism not only as an architectural historian might but also at the deeper and different level—the knowledge that a designer must marshal to absorb that language. His design for the house, called Rowdy Meadow, took the style and hints of Expressionism further than architects in 1908 were able to do, both inside and out; in 2021, we published a book on the house and its collections and are proud that the entire property will someday be a public part of the Cleveland Museum of Art. This style later informed our competition-winning design for the clock in the new Moynihan Train Hall, a small but visible project set at the center of this well-traveled New York crossroads.

Our understanding of history through the eyes of architectural practice has also given us the tools to approach preservation projects in an unorthodox way. In the world of architectural practices that follow the prevailing theories, new—typically modernist—additions

RIGHT
As a counterproposal to
Foster + Partners' modernist
plan of 2013 to displace the
New York Public Library's
historic book stacks, PPA
showed that a new lending
library could be sympathetic
to Carrère & Hastings'
original design. Watercolor
by Anton Glikin.

BELOW
Located below the library's
west terrace, PPA's proposed
vaulted reading room was lit
by clerestory windows and
surrounded by book stacks.
Watercolor by Anton Glikin.

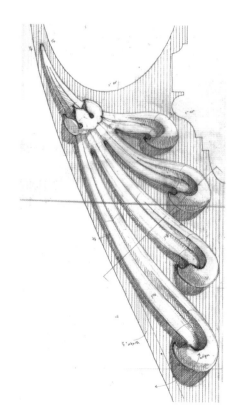

or modifications to landmarks are made to contrast with the original. In our practice, we bring research and imagination to preservation. We believe that our work inside and adding to landmarks can help complete buildings to their highest form, even in the absence of archaeological evidence. Our staff now includes architectural conservationists to fully integrate preservation's best practices into renovations and new construction alike, because enduring buildings are sustainable buildings.

Our research raises the quality of our work for clients, but it also equips us to teach and advocate for better architecture for New York City. Our designs are better for our recognition that we must understand how great architects thought. Understanding the context and history of a site also informs every design and is critical for winning over preservation and planning authorities. We have published books on architects we especially admire—those practitioners of the first half of the twentieth century who had to adapt to the rising tide of modernism, which almost obliterated the core values of the traditional, humanistic approach—harmony, proportion, and beauty. Our books on Harrie T. Lindeberg and the architect brothers John and Eliot Cross have added to our understanding of practices that remain relevant today.

Our advocacy is based on our passion for great buildings that are at the soul of New York City. In 2013, the New York Public Library presented plans by Norman Foster for a new, modernist lending library that would displace the book stacks that occupied the west side of the building designed by Carrère and Hastings. Preservationists, writers, and devotees of the library protested. Our team designed a counterproposal design for a new, larger lending library under an existing terrace. We promoted this design to the board of the library and other New Yorkers to demonstrate that the new library could be sympathetic to the Carrère and Hastings architecture. We also created a website to encourage other architects

ABOVE
The design for PPA's blue-and-yellow guest bedroom for the Kips Bay Showhouse in 2019 was inspired by Schumacher's Le Castellet upholstery fabric with a citron twist.

to propose solutions. We continue to believe that our voice in public debates on preservation, zoning, and other urban issues is amplified when we take the time to think as designers, not just as critics of proposed redevelopments.

Taking these lessons into the classroom, my colleague Anne Walker and I have taught that scholarship is a sound basis not only for creativity but also for advocacy, drawing the students in our seminar at NYU into a close study of history through the study of buildings. To prove that their careful research might have a greater purpose, we required our students to judge each building's worthiness for protection by the New York City Landmarks Preservation Commission. Our students appreciated that learning about architecture as historians required judgment, that not all buildings are equal.

Over the years, I believe that we have also fostered young talent in our practice and inspired others along the way. Turning our knowledge of precedent into the raw material of new, imaginative designs requires the skill of hand drawing to forge an enduring connection between the hand and the mind and the human scale of the design—something that can be lost through keystrokes and computer design. At our firm, these drawings say much about the approach of the designer: Gregory Gilmartin's ink perspective sketches appear as he explains his thinking, revealing a challenge and solving it a few deft strokes; his design drawings, drafted in sharp graphite lines on tracing paper, convey the precision of a design that is fully formed. Eero Schultz, a seasoned designer and accomplished artist in our firm, draws in bold, impressionistic lines in wax pencil. His sketches put one in the place, situating a building on its site with trees and daylight. These views, which seem to sculpt space from the raw materials of architecture, have an ineffable immediacy that balances the more technically correct drawings that follow. Partner Tom Nugent's plans are drafted in strong, bold strokes that express a confident commitment to each design.

Hand drawing endures as the principal medium of our office because it is the best expression of our work. Over the past decade, however, new technologies have transformed the practice of architecture in ways I could not have imagined; accelerating the pace and tools of design has had unforetold consequences for both the profession and the built environment, for better and worse. Our commitment to advancing our practice at the pace of technology has had clear benefits but has taken such an investment that I often joke we are a quasi tech firm. To reconcile history and tradition with industry standards, we have forged our own best practices for digital design. For example, our CAD drawings emulate the best hand-drafted work, not the other way around. The layout of our sheets of drawings follow precedents like original ink-on-vellum drawings by William Adams Delano and Charles A. Platt. For visualization we have adopted SketchUp, Rhino, and Lumion. The resulting drawings and renderings work on screen and on paper. At one end of the spectrum, we show

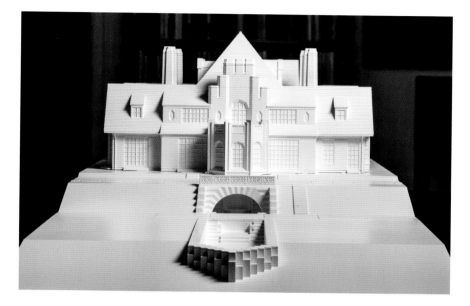

the client a simple line perspective. This puts the focus on the architecture, leaving the textures, colors, furnishings, and materials to actual samples. But we are also capable of producing photo-realistic renderings that show architecture exactly as it would appear in a photograph, fully furnished. Using these tools, we can create animations—even VR walk-throughs—with accurate daylighting and projections of perspectival space.

These programs also feed into our in-house 3D printer. These prints vary from small massing models, which allow quicker studies of a building shape, to full-fledged presentation models that show every brick and windowpane. 3D printing has proven especially helpful in making rapid prototypes of smaller elements—hardware, grilles, railings, and moldings. Though we have always custom-designed these architectural details, 3D printing has opened the door to manufacturing products on a consumer level. In 2014 we began a partnership with Lowe Hardware of Rockland, Maine, on three suites of architectural hardware: city, country, and cubist. Increasing our collaborations with artisans and crafts-men, such as Lowe, has been one of the most rewarding facets of PPA's growth over the past decade, made possible by new design technologies. Adopting programs such as Revit, which is more commonly used for larger and more complex projects than those found in our residential portfolio, has allowed us to broaden our practice into large, commercial work that requires Revit. Within the past six years, we designed two new residential towers in Manhattan, 151 East 78th Street and The Benson on Madison Avenue (see pages 124–29 and 130–35), which would not have been possible for our studio ten years ago.

As most architects do, we work very hard. Looking back at the past decade, we are convinced that the extra effort required by our two tracks—retaining our commitment to history, excellence, and precedent while embracing the newest technologies—is the right formula for continued success. We are a place where you can find a moldy, early seventeenth-century French framing manual and a Beta testing code under the same roof. With digital tools, we have broadened our range of styles; our palate has become more com-plex, more adventurous. And yet our creative process endures, flowing from our library. We keep scholarship alive within our walls, even while challenging ourselves with new project types: onward and upward.

ABOVE LEFT
The Cubist Suite is one of the hardware collections designed by PPA and produced in collaboration with Lowe Hardware in Maine.

ABOVE RIGHT
For Rowdy Meadow, the Czech Cubism–inspired house that PPA designed in Hunting Valley, Ohio, PPA studied the massing of the house using 3D-printed models produced in-house from digital design files.

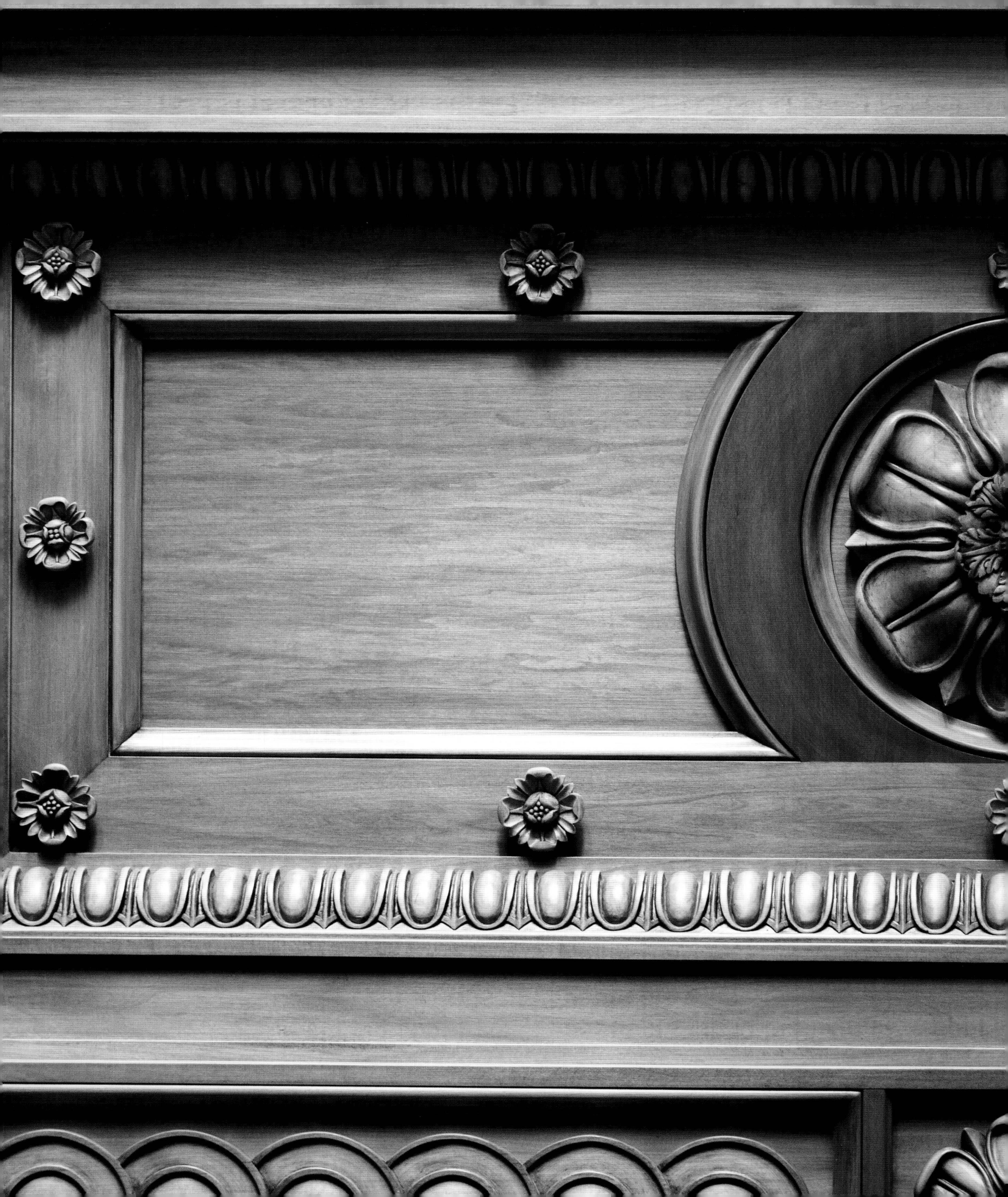

CITY
APARTMENTS
TOWNHOUSES
APARTMENT BUILDINGS

CANDELA DUPLEX

This 4,000-square-foot duplex is located in a landmark Upper East Side building designed by Rosario Candela in 1929. The Italian-born architect was the master of well-laid-out apartments characterized by intricately jigsawed-together spaces that shaped the ideal of the Manhattan apartment in the 1920s. Not only were his apartments luxurious, but his buildings—recognizable by their picturesque rooflines formed by setbacks and terraces on the upper floors—continue to be coveted. In updating this apartment to accommodate a family, PPA stayed true to the spirit of Candela's original scheme while injecting it with new life, through both the architecture and the decorating.

As originally designed, the first floor of the duplex consisted of separate and distinct rooms that opened off the foyer and stair hall. The public rooms—living room, library, and dining room—faced the front of the building, while the kitchen, servants' rooms, and back hall overlooked the rear courtyard. The heavy moldings, gilded wall paneling, and stone of the interiors looked tired and were too elaborate for the clients' taste. To open and refresh the space, PPA added a set of doors between the previously closed-off living room and the new dining room—formerly the library. The doors center on the dining room fireplace, which is itself flanked by mirrored French doors. One set leads to a bar; the other connects to the family room. Decorated by PPA Interiors, the rooms glitter in tones of blue and gold; custom furniture commingles with mid-century and contemporary pieces. The restored floor-to-ceiling windows in the living room draw in natural light, while the blue-lacquered wood paneling, curved walls, and gilded ellipse set into the ceiling give the dining room a cosmopolitan flair. The original dining room was transformed into a large family room with glass pocket

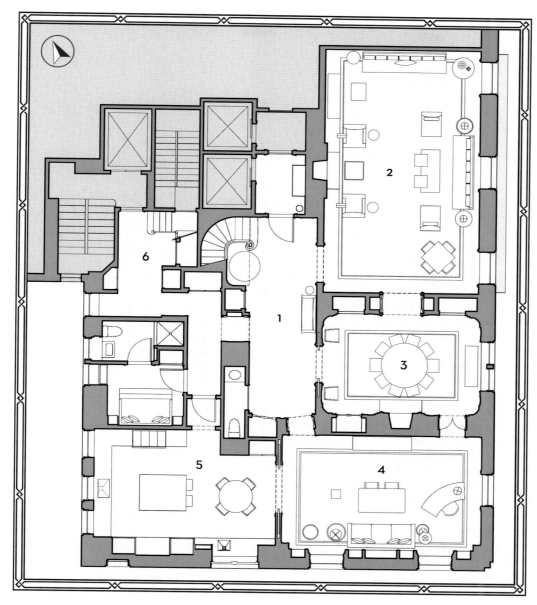

PRECEDING PAGES
New finishes in the paneled dining room include a gilded cove ceiling and light oak floors. The round table is centered on a Calacatta Vagli marble mantel.

OPPOSITE
PPA updated the entrance gallery with a diamond-patterned floor of honed Bardiglio Imperial and Calacatta Extra marble, white-painted paneled walls, and a ceiling lantern by Hervé Van der Straeten. The restored neoclassical railing enhances the curve of the stair.

OVERLEAF LEFT
A Franck Evennou mirror, flanked by Charles Paris sconces, hangs above a fluted Calacatta Vagli marble mantel in the living room.

OVERLEAF RIGHT
Restored full-length windows that were previously truncated by air-conditioning units draw light into the living room. A new cased doorway with a pair of Harmon-hinge doors opens the living room into the dining room.

FLOOR PLAN

The first-floor plan illustrates the connection between the living, dining, and family rooms; glazed pocket doors open the kitchen up to the family room.

1 Gallery and Stair Hall
2 Living Room
3 Dining Room
4 Family Room
5 Kitchen
6 Back Stair Hall

doors that open into the kitchen, perhaps the most-used space in the apartment. The light pouring in from both the family room and the courtyard windows reflects off the kitchen's pale gray ceramic-tile walls, helping to dispel Candela's separation of the apartment's front and back quarters.

Off the main hall, a narrow powder room has been transformed into an event with a vaulted and gilded ceiling, mirrored walls, and decorative fretwork. From the hall, Candela's stair curves up to the bedroom level. Refinished, the original neoclassical wrought-iron railing has been toned down; a new bull's-eye window brings light to and from the kitchen stair directly behind. Upstairs, changes over time had made the plan of the bedroom floor

awkward; one of the original bedrooms had been turned into a dressing room, and doors and closets had been shifted into odd locations. By reworking the existing layout, PPA streamlined the flow of space and incorporated a new, oval-shaped vestibule as an entry point for the reconfigured primary suite. Separated from the children's rooms, the suite's bedroom, small study, his-and-her dressing rooms, and large bath with the tub set under west-facing windows ensure a luxurious privacy. Throughout, the architecture is disciplined—rooms are defined by cornices and moldings—yet the touch is light and much more spare; the modern art on the walls, white oak floors, and neutral-colored rugs also give the traditional spaces a lighter, more contemporary feel.

LEFT
In the kitchen, glossy gray tile and white oak wood floors laid in a herringbone pattern are enlivened by pops of brass and orange.

ABOVE
Glazed pocket doors enable light from the street-facing family room to filter back into the kitchen.

LEFT
A sunlit corner of the family room houses a John Fischer desk and built-in bookshelves.

ABOVE
A set of antique mirrored Harmon-hinge doors in the dining room opens to reveal a bar with a tiger onyx countertop and grained zebrawood cabinets.

OPPOSITE
PPA transformed the apartment's former dining room into a family room with built-in bookshelves and walls clad in raffia.

ABOVE LEFT
In the primary bedroom, a parchment-fronted cabinet stands next to the mantel, painted by Boyd Reath to imitate rainbow onyx and hammered bronze.

LEFT
In the primary bathroom, the honed-marble floor is laid in a chevron pattern.

RIGHT
Decorated in muted colors, the bedroom features a Gracie silk covering the wall behind the bed and curtains that complement the tones of the mantel.

FIFTH AVENUE MAISONETTE

With its own address, this duplex maisonette has a private entrance that opens directly onto Fifth Avenue and Central Park. At only thirty feet wide, the building—designed by Rosario Candela and Walker & Gillette in 1927—feels like a traditional townhouse, but because it extends the length of the lot along the side street, the plan of the apartment is deeper than expected, especially on the second floor. Located across from the Frick Collection, every room has eye-level views of the famed mansion and its gardens. The owners engaged PPA to reimagine the plan and interior architecture, and the firm's interior design team to decorate the 5,000-square-foot apartment.

Before the renovation, the maisonette looked dark and rather dreary. On the first level, the entry vestibule and stair hall connecting the Fifth Avenue entrance, sitting room, and dining room to the lobby of the apartment building were closed off from the rest of the duplex. The kitchen, relegated to the far corner of the plan, felt distant and cloistered. The potential of the large living room on the upper level, stretching the width of the building with views both north and west, sat untapped, and the dark hallway leading back to the bedrooms was long and undefined.

By rearranging walls and widening doorways, PPA flooded the place with western and northern light and reinforced connections between spaces. PPA's décor—a smart, modern amalgam of new custom pieces, special antiques, fresh colors, and Eastern accents reflecting the owners' Asian roots—reinvigorated the traditional interiors. From the inviting sitting room on the first floor, which PPA paneled in a pale waxed oak, arches now lead into the square dining room, papered in a fresh floral chinoiserie print, and the kitchen. PPA complemented the shape of the dining room with circular ceiling moldings and a round, custom-made ebony-and-mahogany

PRECEDING PAGES
Pale waxed-oak paneling with
beaded faux-bois molding
encases the family room;
shutters in the arched window
jambs provide privacy from
the street.

RIGHT
A scalloped handkerchief
vault in white gold leaf floats
over the entrance vestibule
from the lobby.

dining table. The curves echo the gentle archways that open the space to the rest of the apartment. PPA enlarged the kitchen by combining it with an adjacent breakfast room and brightened it with a light palette of fiddleback sycamore cabinetry, teak flooring, and Calacatta marble walls; mirrored window jambs reflect views of the Frick Collection garden. PPA fitted the ceiling of the vestibule between the apartment and the apartment-building lobby with a stylish, scalloped handkerchief vault clad in white gold leaf.

The stair, embellished with a new stylized bronze handrail, curls up to the second-floor landing, where the step-down living room opens to the west. To highlight the luminosity of the French casement windows, PPA lacquered the ceiling and installed a cast-glass paneled mirror on the south wall of the room. With walls sheathed in parchment of the palest apricot, cove moldings, custom furnishings, and Asian pieces and artifacts, PPA transformed what had been a bland space into a sleek, sophisticated room. PPA reconfigured the bedrooms, making them smaller to accommodate additional closet space; they are decorated as luxuriously as hotel suites, reflecting the owner's taste as a hotelier. To brighten the previously dark and bland bedroom hallway, PPA incorporated a barrel-vaulted ceiling, adding both height and architectural character, and lacquered it a brilliant white.

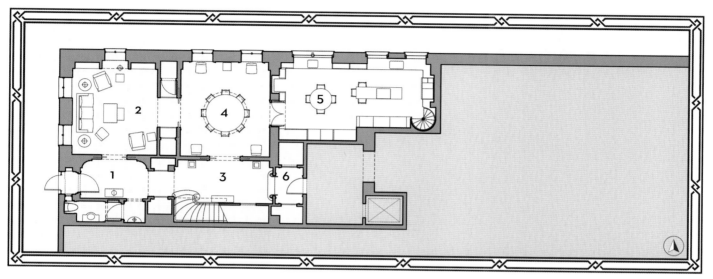

1ST-FLOOR PLAN

PPA opened up the plan, connecting the spaces with wide, arched pocket doors.

1 Foyer
2 Family Room
3 Stair Hall
4 Dining Room
5 Kitchen
6 Entrance vestibule from the lobby

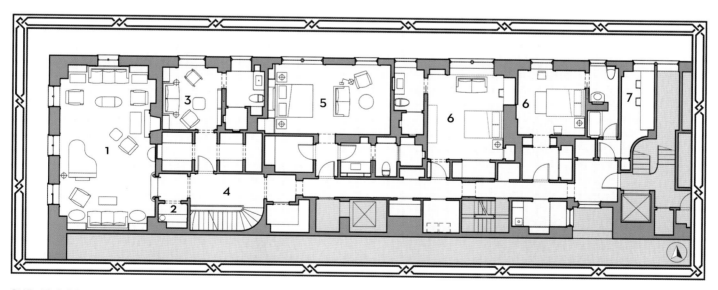

2ND-FLOOR PLAN

Upstairs, the bedroom hallway is paneled with fluted plaster joined by a barrel-vaulted ceiling.

1 Living Room
2 Bar
3 Study
4 Upper Stair Hall
5 Primary Bedroom
6 Bedroom
7 Office

ABOVE
The view from the front door on Fifth Avenue extends through the barrel-vaulted vestibule and stair hall to the arched entrance of the vestibule that connects the maisonette to the building's public lobby.

OPPOSITE
The curve of the bronze stair rail echoes the wide, arched doorway of the dining room, which PPA wrapped in a jade-green chinoiserie wallpaper.

OPPOSITE

On the first floor, an enfilade of arched pocket doors connects the family room, dining room, and kitchen. In the dining room, the circular ceiling molding is embellished with a band of beaded trim gilded in silver leaf.

ABOVE

The kitchen was enlarged and brightened with a light palette of fiddleback sycamore cabinetry, teak flooring, Calacatta marble walls, and mirrored window jambs reflecting views of the Frick Collection garden.

LEFT
A vestibule with fluted-plaster walls and gold leaf ceiling leads into the second-floor living room overlooking Central Park.

OPPOSITE
PPA decorated the living room with creamy leather walls, custom furnishings, and the clients' Asian collections. A lacquered ceiling and a mirror-paneled wall on the south end of the room enhance the effect of the luminous French casement windows.

ABOVE
A bar paneled in brushed oak opens to the fluted-plaster-lined vestibule, which leads into the living room.

OPPOSITE
A second-floor study paneled in Mozambique wood opens to the upstairs hall.

OPPOSITE
A guest bedroom with a striking red-lacquered ceiling and stenciled border is decorated with Asian-inspired furnishings.

ABOVE
The primary bedroom features handmade silk wallpaper and a Fortuny print on the loveseat.

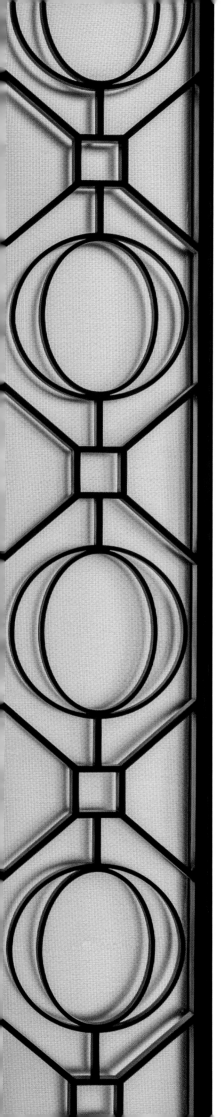

EAST SIDE APARTMENT

As first advertised in the *New York Times*, this full-floor apartment, located in an early rental building designed by J. E. R. Carpenter in 1914, has "a spaciousness suggestive of the famous country homes." Developed by S. Fullerton Weaver to entice townhouse dwellers to embrace apartment living, each apartment featured large rooms with Brazilian walnut floors, five fireplaces, seven-foot-wide hallways, and ample servants' quarters. Apart from 1970s-era bathroom interventions, the bones of this 6,500-square-foot apartment were intact when PPA came onto the project. However, in addition to the advantages of a Carpenter-designed building—bright, expansive rooms, well-planned spaces, and pre-war architectural details—there were drawbacks by today's standards: long, dark hallways and a rabbit warren of small service spaces and servants' rooms.

The owners entrusted PPA with revamping the Carpenter plan for modern living. In its original condition, the great entry gallery opening into the public rooms was dark and underwhelming, and the bedroom hallway seemed endless. In the public area, PPA opened the living room to the dining room; a pair of double doors and a pair of Doric piers with softly rounded corners delineate the salon, an intermediary space that divides the extra-long living room into two open areas better scaled for furniture groupings. By moving the air-conditioning units from the windows of the front rooms and bedrooms, PPA was able to restore the arches on the limestone façade of the building, which had been compromised by HVAC grilles.

PPA worked with interior designer David Kleinberg to bring a stylized glamour to the interiors, transforming the entry gallery into a bright, lofty space enhanced by a deep oval ceiling molding, restrained wall paneling, and a linen-beige limestone floor inlaid with a geometric pattern of gray onyx and Black Forest marble. Inspired by the ironwork of Louis Sullivan,

the glazed entry door is overlaid with a screen wrought in a circle-and-square pattern, a motif worked into other metalwork designs in the apartment. Black-lacquered interior doors inlaid with stainless-steel-and-brass geometric patterns tie the front quarters together, at the same time creating a sophisticated balance of light and dark. The fluted mantels and stylized moldings reinforce this bold Art Deco aesthetic. To showcase their art collection, the owners wanted to maximize the ceiling heights and incorporate attractive lighting throughout the apartment. By aligning doorways and fireplaces—all slightly off-center in the Carpenter plan—PPA brought a symmetrical order that in turn produced pronounced and identifiable places to hang art, lit by inconspicuous fixtures that blend with the white walls and ceilings.

Pocket doors separate the dining room from the breakfast room; the doors can be closed when entertaining but allow light to filter into the rear of the apartment when open. The kitchen and breakfast room, once a sequence of small, dark rooms, have been brightened with white cabinetry, light terrazzo floors, and Calacatta Lincoln marble walls. The gold trim, range hood, and screen of leaf and circle motifs on *verre églomisé* by Miriam Ellner create an unexpected wow factor.

PPA broke up the length of the wide bedroom hallway, giving each room-like section a specific architectural character. Off the front hall, a formal symmetrical vestibule accesses the powder room; beyond stretches a section of hall with a white-painted, barrel-vaulted ceiling that leads to the bedrooms. A groin-vaulted midsection forms the junction of a spur that accesses the playroom and kitchen quarters to the south and a guest suite to the north. The hallway terminates at a vaulted octagonal vestibule with floral bas-relief wall panels, which is the entry and main circulation point of the primary suite. It opens into a bright corner bedroom, as well as an anigre wood–paneled dressing room with a laylight and his-and-her bathrooms luxuriously finished in Zebrino Light and Calacatta Striato marble.

TOP
The piers between the salon and adjoining living room have softly rounded corners.

ABOVE
In the gallery, open patterns in the moldings conceal the air-supply vents.

RIGHT
A groin-vaulted section of the long, wide bedroom hallway is detailed with thin, rib-like moldings and floorboards laid in a square pattern.

RIGHT
On the west wall of the gallery, the entry is flanked by a pair of black-lacquered doors inlaid with geometric patterns of stainless steel and brass. One leads to the playroom and kitchen wing; the other, to the bedroom hall.

OPPOSITE
A pair of Doric piers divides the large living room into two spaces. Beyond, two sets of black-lacquered doors open into the dining room.

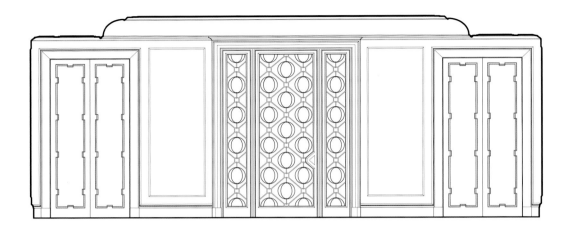

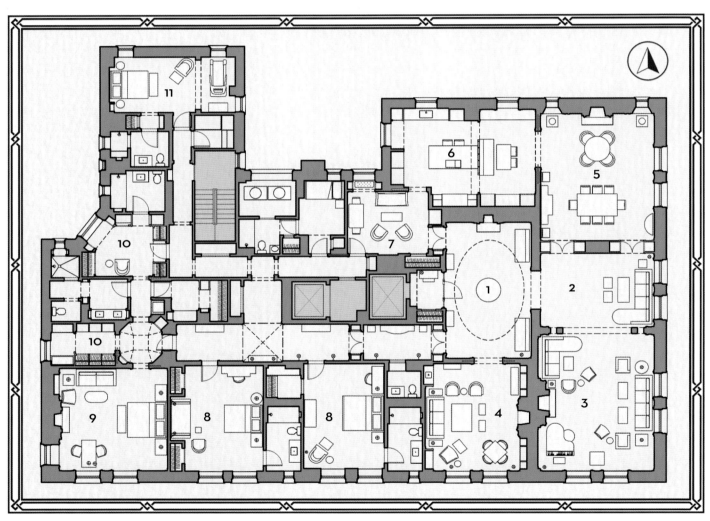

FLOOR PLAN

PPA aligned openings and brought a symmetrical order to the rooms.

1 Gallery
2 Salon
3 Living Room
4 Study
5 Dining Room
6 Kitchen
7 Playroom
8 Bedroom
9 Primary Bedroom
10 Dressing Room
11 Guest Room

ABOVE
Eastern- and southern-facing windows flood the living room with natural light.

OPPOSITE
Restrained architectural details and a fluted-plaster mantel reflect an Art Deco aesthetic.

OVERLEAF LEFT
In the walnut-paneled study, the bar is framed by a cast-bronze strip with a geometrical motif that relates to the metalwork throughout the apartment.

OVERLEAF RIGHT
A Grigio Scuro marble mantel is set against a mirrored chimney breast.

OPPOSITE AND ABOVE
The kitchen, once a sequence of small, dark rooms, is brightened
with white cabinetry, light terrazzo floors, Calacatta Lincoln marble
walls, and gold accents. A screen of leaf and circle motifs on *verre
églomisé* by Miriam Ellner echoes the design on the entrance door.

LEFT
The walls of the primary
bedroom are upholstered in
wool sateen, folded to create
vertical lines.

ABOVE
A cast-glass bolection
mantel reflects light from
the windows.

EAST SIDE APARTMENT

61

ART DECO ON THE RIVER

Sutton Place, East End Avenue, and Beekman Place grew into fashionable residential districts in the late 1920s as New York developers began to capitalize on the city's riverfront. This apartment is in an Art Deco building from 1929 designed by Sloan & Robertson and Corbett, Harrison & MacMurray and built by a conglomerate headed by David Milton, the first husband of Abby Aldrich Rockefeller. PPA's redesign sought to recapture the Jazz Age exuberance that characterized modern classicism during the 1920s. For the décor, Victoria Hagan's rich use of lacquers, parchment, contrasting colors, and textures underscore this Art Deco spirit.

Originally designed to be the lower floor of an expansive duplex, the apartment plan was substantially modified by the developers after the Depression hit and the demand for huge suites dried up. The entrance gallery—once intended to house a grand stair—was oddly oversized with a window awkwardly situated in a corner. The rooms—particularly the living room—were also oversized, intended to accommodate a five-bedroom duplex. The plan posed a challenge: how to reweave the spaces into an elegantly proportioned plan.

Measuring twenty-nine by fourteen feet, the gallery was dark and hollow, whereas the thirty-eight-foot-long living room with exposures on three sides was incredibly bright. It hovered wonderfully over the water, creating the sensation that one was standing high up on the deck of an ocean liner at sea. Responding to the client's passion for the era of ocean liners, PPA ran with this notion and evoked the glamorous interiors of the period's fabled steamships in its design, creating the semblance of a salon on a 1930s Cunard ocean liner to set off Hagan's comfortable yet stylish seating arrangements. While PPA's architecture is pared down, the high-gloss white ceilings and mirrored window jambs set at angles bounce light and views of the bustling East River, Brooklyn, and Queens throughout the room. PPA's rosewood fireplace mantel steps up the chimney breast, its dark sheen radiant against the cream-colored parchment panels covering the walls. And, with the relocation of radiators, access to the windows is immediate and unimpeded, emphasizing the floating quality of the space.

The rooms along the south-facing window wall—the library, primary suite, and dining room—did not change much in size, but the oversized gallery underwent a dramatic transformation. PPA shifted the entrance into the apartment from the elevator hall so that it now angles toward the riverfront living room and forms one of the short walls of a new octagonal-shaped gallery. In this small space, PPA sought visual impact, treating every surface to produce a dazzling effect, especially at night. Together, the black-and-white-stenciled floor, alabaster faux-shagreen walls, black-lacquered doors with stylized metal grilles, and stepped ceiling moldings celebrate the crisp geometry of Art Deco design. Meanwhile, its reduction in size—half that of the original gallery—gave PPA space to tuck in extra closets

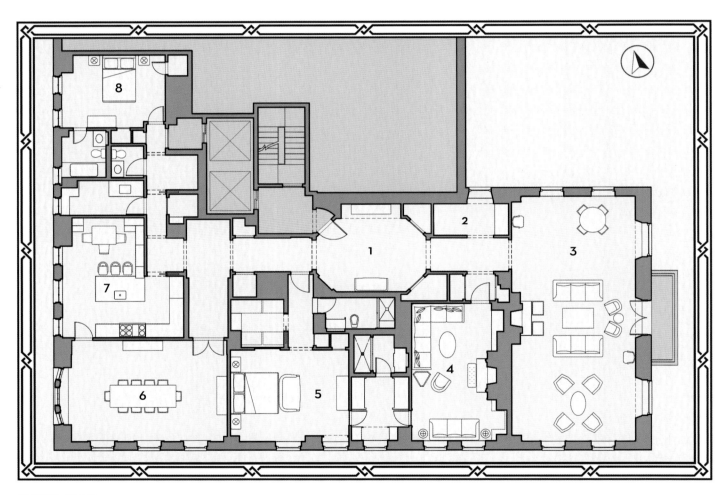

FLOOR PLAN

PPA transformed the plan of the apartment, which had originally been designed as the lower floor of a duplex.

1 Gallery
2 Bar
3 Living Room

4 Study
5 Primary Bedroom
6 Dining Room

7 Kitchen
8 Guest Room

and vestibules and funnel circulation toward the living room past a charming nook with a window seat and bar.

Axial hallways radiating from the octagonal gallery access the public and private areas of the apartment, tying the public rooms together and tucking the primary suite away in cosseted privacy. One wide hallway extends west past the primary bedroom to the dining room. At its end, a black-lacquered paneled wall is embellished with metalwork salvaged from a historic interior in River House—the period's masterpiece Art Deco apartment building—that PPA reproduced as new ornament; pocket doors open to the kitchen on one side and a guest room on the other. Lacquered a rich navy blue, the dining room incorporates a mirrored wall framed by a stainless-steel echelon, or stepped, molding, designed from scratch in keeping with 1929 taste, that reflects city views from the large, west-facing bay window. The adjacent kitchen, with ash cabinetry and a black-and-white-striped terrazzo floor, was designed as a luxuriously paneled room; the custom-designed glass-and-steel range hood is lit from within, creating a glow.

ABOVE
PPA designed the sleek rosewood fireplace mantel in an echelon, or stepped, form; its dark sheen boldly contrasts the cream-colored parchment panels on the walls.

OPPOSITE
With three exposures, the living room seems to hover over the water, creating the sensation that one is standing on a ship's deck. Though PPA's architecture is pared down, the high-gloss white ceilings and mirrored window jambs set at angles bounce light and views of the bustling East River around the room.

ABOVE
With ash cabinetry and a black-and-white-striped terrazzo floor, the kitchen was designed as a luxuriously paneled room.

RIGHT
In the dining room, a mirrored wall framed with a stainless-steel echelon molding reflects the deep blue-lacquered walls and the large west-facing bay window.

LADIES' MILE TRIPLEX

During the late 1800s, Fifth Avenue below 23rd Street was transformed from a residential brownstone district into a fashionable area of upscale department stores and shops. Developers lined the thoroughfare, coined Ladies' Mile, with a series of new and impressive Beaux-Arts and other revival-style commercial and loft buildings and promoted it to women as a strip they could patronize unaccompanied by men. Located on a prominent corner site, the building that houses this colorful triplex was historically occupied by an upscale grocery store, an art lithography publisher, and various shops for hats, pianos, linens, curtains, and jewelry. Built in phases by two different developers and architects (Robert Maynicke, 1897; Henry Edwards Ficken, 1899), the building elegantly curves at the corner and rises twelve stories, culminating in a prominent and richly embellished cupola capped by a copper dome—an architectural flourish that sets its exterior apart from the others on the avenue.

When the building was converted into condominiums in 2007, the interiors were completely stripped and reconfigured into bland apartments with uninspired plans comprised of sheetrock-walled rooms. The clients, a couple with three grown children, were initially drawn to a two-bedroom top-floor apartment with rooftop terraces and a standout feature: the beautiful cupola, in which the developer had inserted a primary bedroom and an oddly organized bathroom above. Combining the space with the adjacent apartment—a smaller duplex—to form a 4,400-square-foot residence, they commissioned PPA and Katie Ridder Interiors to redress the lost character and charm of the interiors and bring out the potential of the architectural elements, particularly the two-story cupola.

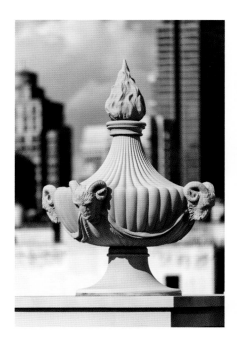  

PPA organized the combined plan around an octagonally shaped formal entry hall that Ridder lacquered a deep blue and lined with custom *verre églomisé* panels by Miriam Ellner. Retaining the staircases on both sides of the apartment, PPA placed the bedrooms on the eastern end and the public rooms to the west. From the entry hall, PPA opened new axes to create sightlines through the stair hall to the kitchen and from the main stair to the living area, which is bowed on one side to mirror the curvature of the dining room bay at the corner of the building. In the spirit of a contemporary loft, the living/dining space flows seamlessly into the newly enlarged kitchen, transitioning from oak floors and honey-hued oak paneling in the former to white oak cabinetry in the latter. The more intimate peacock blue–lacquered study with millwork and built-in bookshelves is accessed through pocket doors in the living area. Three bedrooms, connecting baths, and a laundry room comprise the east wing of the apartment, where a stair leads up to the primary suite and a private terrace. Featuring bespoke window casings, crown moldings, and millwork, all the bedrooms are comfortable and graciously scaled; the bathrooms are sumptuously clad in various kinds of marble, including Calacatta Borghini, Rosa Aurora, and Paonazzo.

While the interiors were undergoing a total overhaul, the renovation of the cupola turned into a major project in its own right; its distinctive architectural embellishments of galvanized steel and zinc—elaborate window enframements, swags, and acanthus leaves—had deteriorated beyond repair. On the interior, a flagpole sat atop a low-set beam, preventing full use of the space. Working with engineer Donald Friedman and preservation architects Jan Hird Pokorny Associates, PPA re-created the massively scaled exterior architectural details out of heavy, pressed and brake-formed copper sheet and painstakingly assembled them off-site before hoisting them into place. With specific treatment and substrate preparation, the exterior was painted a bright sandy color, evoking the building's original terra-cotta finish and blending with the lower façade. The installation of a new support system behind the internal dome that PPA constructed freed the top room from the obstructive steel beam.

ABOVE
PPA's model of the cupola shows a section of the two-tiered interior.

RIGHT
The original shell of the cupola was in disrepair, requiring complete reconstruction. Under the supervision of consultant Jan Hird Pokorny Associates, more than a hundred custom dies were fabricated to stamp replicas of the original historic details in copper. The pressed and brake-formed copper cladding consists of thousands of individual pieces, painstakingly assembled off-site. The copper was then painted to match the terra-cotta masonry of the building's façade as it appeared in 1893.

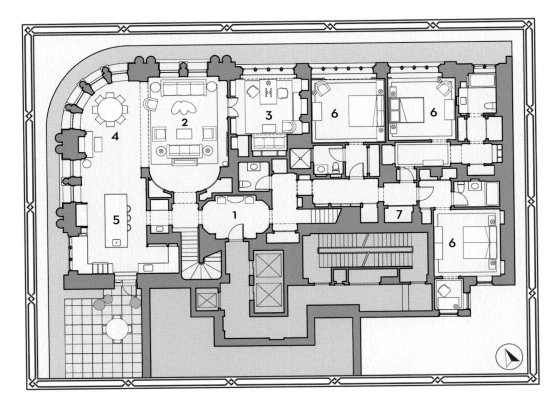

12TH-FLOOR PLAN

The plan combined two separate duplex apartments.

1 Gallery
2 Living Room
3 Study
4 Dining Bay
5 Kitchen
6 Bedroom
7 Laundry Room

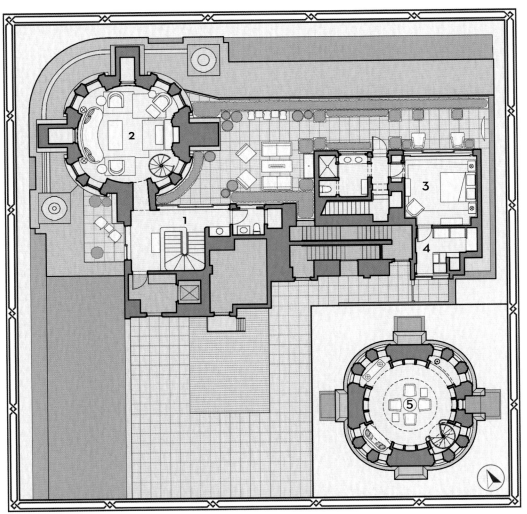

13TH-FLOOR PLAN

Separate stairs access the cupola and the primary suite.

1 Stair Hall
2 Family Room
3 Primary Bedroom
4 Dressing Room
5 Library

This collaboration among architects, interior designers, preservationists, and engineers produced the triplex's most outstanding feature. A light, modern stairwell with a sinuous bronze handrail and inset details curls up from the apartment's first floor to a sunny landing at the base of the cupola that opens into the perfectly round, pale blue entertainment room, illuminated by four sets of large, double-hung wood windows. The ceiling reinforces the circular shape of the room with molded spokes that radiate out to the window bays. In one of the bays, PPA incorporated an elegant bronze stair that spirals up to a cozy library lined with millwork for books and artifacts and furnished with custom sofas that Ridder designed to fit the shape of the window alcoves lit by bull's-eye windows. Above the cornice line, the white-painted dome floats overhead, made bright by four additional bull's-eyes at the attic level. Adorned with great scrolling brackets and swags, rosettes, acanthus leaves, beads, berries, Ionic capitals, and exquisite urns ornamented with rams' heads. PPA's new cupola is resplendent in its restored detail, prominently marking this curved street wall on Ladies' Mile.

ABOVE
The oak-clad kitchen includes a PPA-designed range hood with textured art glass and a polished-nickel frame. The island rests on a granite border.

OPPOSITE
The peacock-blue–lacquered study features a Verde Bamboo stone bolection mantel, oval ceiling molding, and a book-lined niche. A bronze frieze with a Greek-key design disguises the air-supply vent.

OPPOSITE
On the ceiling of the family room, paneled segments radiate out to the window bays like spokes, reflecting and reinforcing the circular shape of the room.

ABOVE LEFT
A solid-bronze spiral stair with elongated, guilloche-like balusters in one of the window bays connects the family room to the circular library above. The cast-glass bolection mantel reflects the light from the surrounding windows.

ABOVE RIGHT
On the second floor of the cupola, oculus windows illuminate each of the four bays in the library. High above the coved cornice, four oculus windows wash light over the dome.

MUSEUM MILE DUPLEX

The owners—a young family of four—were attracted to this apartment because its two floors and stair created the feeling of a house. Located across Fifth Avenue from the Metropolitan Museum of Art, it occupies high floors in an Italian Renaissance–style building designed and developed in 1925 by the Fred F. French Company, a leading real estate investor and builder in the city at that time. Though the clients liked the character and structure of its traditional architecture, they also wanted something less formal, more modern, and with an open, flowing plan that would create a comfortable and functional backdrop for their lifestyle. The owners brought on interior designer Steven Gambrel to layer PPA's new architectural framework—which entailed a gut renovation of the 5,000-square-foot suite—with an effortless mix of patterns, textures, colors, and scales.

A cramped, straight stair had awkwardly merged what had originally been two simplexes into a duplex. The layout of the first floor was a classic seven, while the upper floor—a portion of the original upstairs apartment—contained several more bedrooms. For an apartment of its size, the public rooms were underwhelming, and the corner room on each floor—key real estate with southern and western exposures—was occupied by a secondary bedroom. PPA's challenge was to give the plan a logical flow, which entailed reconfiguring all the rooms and realigning the entrances to the main spaces to provide clear and open views from one to the next. PPA repositioned the living room to the south corner of the lower floor, affording views of the Met and Central Park, and relocated the three family bedrooms upstairs, placing the primary suite on the corner. Forgoing the traditional dining room, PPA incorporated the dining area into the newly enlarged gallery at the center of the plan, featuring walls lined with bronze-framed *verre églomisé* panels, high-gloss chocolate-colored doors, and an antique fireplace; a circular molding in the ceiling

PRECEDING PAGES
Doubling as a dining room,
the enlarged gallery at the
center of the apartment
is enhanced with bronze-
framed *verre églomisé*
panels, high-gloss chocolate-
colored doors, a round
ceiling molding, and fumed
antique-oak floors laid in a
herringbone pattern.

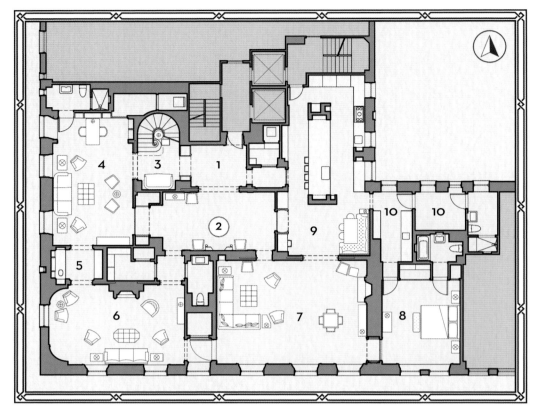

FLOOR PLAN

PPA redesigned the first-floor plan of the duplex to organize the major public rooms around an ample gallery.

1 Foyer	5 Bar	8 Guest Room
2 Gallery	6 Living Room	9 Kitchen
3 Stair Hall	7 Family Room	10 Pantry
4 Library		

accentuates the symmetry of the space. Throughout the lower level, fumed antique-oak floors laid in a bold herringbone pattern add an unexpected and contemporary touch. To emphasize the connection from one space to the next, PPA created an enfilade of rooms along the Fifth Avenue street wall: the living room, sheathed in pale pink Venetian plaster, a windowed bar, and a comfortable, welcoming library with built-in bookshelves, high-gloss blue ceiling beams, and coral-colored doors. PPA combined the ancillary service spaces into one large kitchen with a huge center island and walls clad in a glossy gray ceramic tile; wide sliding doors connect it to an informal family room paneled in knotty pine. The former dining room has been turned into the guest bedroom.

PPA removed the existing stair, which had been perfunctorily tucked away in a vestibule and led right into a bedroom above when the floors were first combined. Now a prominent feature in the apartment, the new curving stair, with a stylized railing accentuating its curvature, swoops up under a circular laylight into an oval-shaped hall leading to the three family bedrooms. With a flair reminiscent of the work of legendary interior decorator Dorothy Draper, the stairwell and hall are plastered in blue, a high-gloss paint of the deepest brown accents the doors and paneling, niches showcase art, and inventive hardware recalls the classical roots of prewar apartment design.

LEFT
Replacing a straight-run stair installed in the 1980s, when the two floors were combined into a duplex, PPA's new stair becomes the pivot of the design, its stylized wrought-iron railing accentuating its curve.

ABOVE
Beneath a circular laylight, the stair curves up into an oval hallway on the second floor.

LEFT
In the library, ceiling beams and moldings set off a reading area with built-in bookshelves. A strigilate frieze in a ceiling beam masks the air-supply vent.

ABOVE
A windowed bar of cerused, rift-sawn white oak connects the library and living room.

ABOVE
Small service rooms were combined into a large kitchen with glossy gray ceramic tile walls and an island with a Calacatta Gold marble countertop.

RIGHT
Paneled in a warm Scottish knotty pine, the family room is centered on a marble fireplace surround and opens into the kitchen through wide sliding pocket doors.

ABOVE
On the upstairs stair landing, a niche that mirrors a door to the bedroom hall provides a place for a sculpture. The moldings are spare but enlivened by Steven Gambrel's bold palette.

OPPOSITE
In the sitting area of the primary bedroom, the moldings and paneling were designed to reflect the classical roots of prewar apartment house design but with a greater degree of invention and boldness.

ABOVE
In the first-floor guest room, a variegated-green paneled wall conceals a series of doors to the bathroom, closets, and kitchen area.

OPPOSITE
A pair of paneled Harmon-hinge doors open into the guest room from the family room.

TWO TOWNHOUSES INTO ONE

Combining two landmarked, six-story limestone townhouses in the Upper East Side Historic District into a single 22,000-square-foot house was a complex undertaking. The first, a three-bay Beaux-Arts townhouse built by Foster & Gade in 1913, resembles a fragment of Haussmann's Paris with its wrought-iron balconies and mansard roof tucked behind a stone balustrade. To the east, the adjoining townhouse, designed by the Beaux-Arts-trained Harry Allan Jacobs in 1921, features a heroically scaled serliana that lit the space behind (in which theatrical impresario Martin Beck, founder of the Palace and Martin Beck Theaters, staged private performances). When purchased, the neo-French house had been divided up into apartments and the Jacobs house had continued as a single-family home; both had deteriorated over time, inside and out.

Carefully cleaned and restored, each limestone façade was brought back to its original expression. On the Foster & Gade house, the crumbling stone balconies were reconstructed, and replica wood window frames were installed. Next door, the wrought-iron balconies and decorative castings were repaired, and the steel casements were re-created in bronze. At sidewalk level, PPA restored Jacobs's ornate bronze entry doors and designed a new planted areaway with complementary railings for the adjoining house. Built to the rear lot line, the garden elevation of both houses was a jumble of additions and fire escapes. Now, clad in a period-appropriate white-glazed brick, the backyard elevation is flush, with new windows that relate to the historic exteriors.

Behind the two landmarked façades, the original buildings were demolished and rebuilt, intricately weaving together spatial and aesthetic clues from the exterior. Different volumes and their attendant scales and expressions of architectural detail form a multi-level—almost imbricated—interior.

PRECEDING PAGES

In the curiosity room, set several steps below the living room, built-in marquetry bookcases flank an Amazonite mantel carved in a faceted-diamond pattern.

At the front of the house, new plans correspond with the landmarked exteriors: the serliana window of the east building's façade informed the generous piano nobile that now extends to the rear of the house. Through a theatrical pair of arches flanking the grand staircase, the ample volume blooms in the formal living and dining rooms, culminating in a proportionate triplet of arched windows overlooking the rear of the house. Inspired by the relative delicacy of the west building's façade, its front interior is more precious in scale, with short runs of stairs linking together a "collector's cabinet" of intimate spaces. Shifts in floor levels from one property to the other were gradually manipulated: at the front of the house, nine levels are spread among five floors, while at the center and back of the house, five levels span five floors.

With Jacobs's monumental façade designated as the formal entrance, a ceremonial procession progresses from a vaulted entry vestibule, through a rotunda laid in a pattern of Pietra Serena and Calacatta Gold marble, to a wide central stair leading up to the second floor. Lit by a laylight, the lofty, vaulted stair hall anchors the combined buildings. Another, east–west, axis connects the stair hall and formal portion of the house to the family quarters and another stair

SECTION

A view through the house looking south shows the realignment of the connections between the two houses.

SECTION

A transverse section looking west shows the loft of the piano nobile and the stair hall that anchors the space.

extending the full height of the house. Bedrooms, a family room, and a top-lit living hall complete the upper floors. The primary suite is on the top level, creating a private rooftop oasis with a bedroom, powder room, large bath, dressing room, and terrace. In the basement, PPA excavated below the foundation to incorporate a 75-foot-long blue glass mosaic lap pool and a gym.

The great scale of the rooms welcomed a robust hand in designing the architectural details, from the intricate scrolling acanthus moldings in the rotunda to the rusticated base of the stair hall. The client, an artist and his family, brought on decorator Giovanna Bianco, who vibrantly layered the interiors with richly hued rugs and wallpaper, eclectic furnishings, and oversized chandeliers. Throughout, intricate mahogany woodwork and wainscoting, paired with Bianco's décor, give rise to a sequence of spaces that celebrate pattern, color, and ornament—a modern-day interpretation of the Aesthetic movement of the 1880s. In the living room, the American walnut coffered ceiling, based on Roman precedents (such as the Palazzo Farnese) and hand carved with rosettes, egg-and-dart motifs, and acanthus leaves, soars dramatically overhead, its woodwork complemented by bracketed bull's-eye windows and pedimented doorways. The wainscoted and ooffered-ceilinged dining room opens into the kitchen, which is clad in lustrous, deep red ceramic tile and mahogany cabinetry to match. Attic-story windows provide unexpected views from room to room: a fanlight in an upstairs office overlooks the dining room, while bull's-eye windows in the third-floor study provide a view of the intricately carved ceiling of the living room. In the curiosity room, set several steps below the living room, marquetry built-in bookcases flank an Amazonite mantel carved in a faceted-diamond pattern. The level of detail extends to the multiple bedroom levels, also brimming with color and interest. Creating a cohesive family home from two very different buildings with complex spatial relationships challenged PPA but also offered the chance to develop an architectural language reflective of the varying scale and character of these two important Upper East Side townhouses.

ABOVE LEFT
A heroically scaled serliana anchors the façade of the house designed by Harry Allan Jacobs in 1921.

ABOVE CENTER
The façade was carefully cleaned and restored, and the failing stone elements were reconstructed.

ABOVE RIGHT
PPA repaired the wrought-iron balconies and decorative castings and re-created the steel casements in bronze.

ABOVE LEFT
A rotunda with a geometrically patterned floor of Pietra Serena and Calacatta Gold marble connects the entry vestibule to a wide central stair.

ABOVE RIGHT
The vaulted entry vestibule features arched niches and a glazed front door with bronze ironwork, which PPA restored.

OPPOSITE
In the lofty central stair, PPA incorporated a rusticated plaster base, crown moldings in the shape of acanthus leaves, and a stylized wrought-iron balustrade. It occupies the core of the house and connects to the family stair beyond.

LEFT
In the upper stair hall, the vaulted ceiling is punctuated by a laylight with decorative ironwork, and the wall moldings create frames for hanging artwork.

OPPOSITE
On the upper level, the tall arched doorway into the living room reflects the central arch of the serliana facing the street.

OVERLEAF LEFT
PPA designed the coffered American walnut ceiling, which is based on Roman precedents. It features hand-carved rosettes, egg-and-dart motifs, and acanthus leaves.

OVERLEAF RIGHT
The double-height volumes of the public rooms called for robust architectural details, including the pedimented doorway and upper-level bull's-eye windows in the living room.

ABOVE
A view from the living room
into the curiosity room.
The doorway is framed by
a mahogany pediment.

RIGHT
The doorway between
the curiosity room and the
living room is set several
steps up, showing the
connection between the
two historic houses.

OPPOSITE
The scale of the serliana
informed the pair of arches
that flank the stair hall.

ABOVE
The kitchen, with mahogany
cabinetry and deep red
ceramic tile, opens into the
dining room at the rear of
the house.

ABOVE
The delicacy of the house designed by Foster & Gade inspired more intimately scaled interiors, including a small office with a fanlight overlooking the dining room.

OPPOSITE
From a third-floor study, a bull's-eye window provides an unexpected view of the top of the living room.

OPPOSITE
Mahogany woodwork and multi-patterned walls give an upstairs vestibule and bedroom an Aesthetic movement quality.

ABOVE
On the top floor of the Foster & Gade–designed house, a child's bedroom tucks into the slope of the roofline.

GREENWICH VILLAGE TOWNHOUSE

Located in the heart of the Greenwich Village Historic District, this red-brick Italianate rowhouse was built in 1856–57 as part of a unified street wall by mason-builder Linus Scudder, an important local developer of that period. Extensive modifications had compromised its architectural integrity, as the house had been subdivided into studio apartments, the stoop eliminated in favor of a basement entrance, and a fourth floor added. Though landmarked, the original details and historic charm of the façade had been either stripped or damaged, and the interior stair, along with beams and other materials inside, were unsalvageable.

In resuscitating the dilapidated rowhouse, PPA restored the façade to its historic form while building an entirely new 5,500-square-foot structure behind it. On the front elevation, PPA repointed the brick and resurfaced the brownstone masonry, restoring the cornice and the lintels—the only original elements that remained. Fortunately, two of the brick rowhouses in Scudder's 1857 strip of six had been minimally altered and provided PPA with a template for the original details: a high, wide stoop, cast-iron stair and areaway railings embellished with a wreath motif that was favored by the Victorians, curved stone eyebrow lintels over windows, a segmental arch entrance frame, and French windows on the main floor.

On the parlor level, PPA reestablished the front entrance with its segmental arch, heavy moldings, and recessed outer doors surrounded by rope moldings, reinstalled the French windows, and designed new paneled and intricately carved outer doors. The rear façade was restored, much of it by using matching brick-and-bond work with mortar compatible with the historic masonry. PPA designed a new cast-iron spiral stair

111

PRECEDING PAGES
The rear parlor is centered on
a new classical stone mantel
and enhanced by elaborate
plaster crown moldings.

ABOVE
The intact elements of the
neighboring rowhouses
served as a template for the
lost details of the landmarked
street façade.

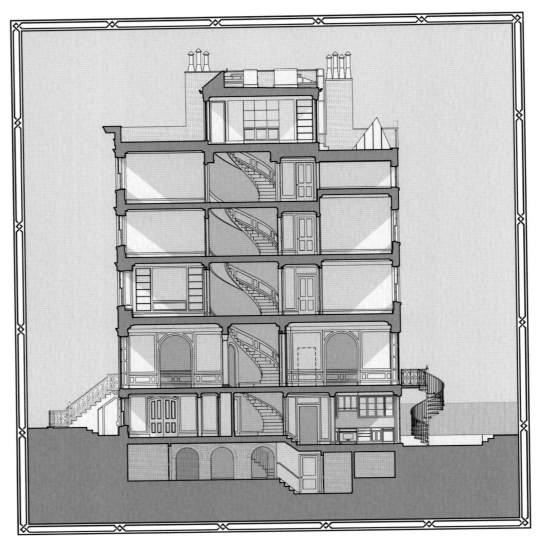

SECTION

PPA's new stair spirals up at the center of the house.

from the parlor floor to the garden, which was designed by Madison Cox, with areaway railings matching the ironwork in the front. Though the footprint of the house remained unchanged, PPA added a penthouse flanked by terraces to the north and south, permitted by the Landmarks Preservation Commission because it was set back and undetectable from the street.

PPA collaborated with expert engineers to weave in all of the modern systems that make the new house behind the landmarked façade comfortable. Following the original footprint and the irregularities of the Greenwich Village lot, the new structure had to be built out of square. For design inspiration, PPA studied the Victorian-style architecture of the mid-to-late nineteenth century, including the all-important pattern books used by the builders of that era such as Samuel Sloan's *The Model Architect* (1852), as well as the *Robert J. Milligan House Parlor* (1854–56), a period room at the Brooklyn Museum. Typically, brownstones comprised a straight stair that ascended against the party wall and was aligned with the front entrance and stoop. PPA centered the reconfigured plan on a skylit round stair that

CLOCKWISE FROM TOP LEFT
The new railing incorporates a wreath motif that was popular during the Victorian era. PPA re-created the stoop and intricately detailed railings. New paneled and carved outer doors were installed. In the rear, a new cast-iron spiral stair accessing the garden and new areaway railings were designed to match the ironwork in front.

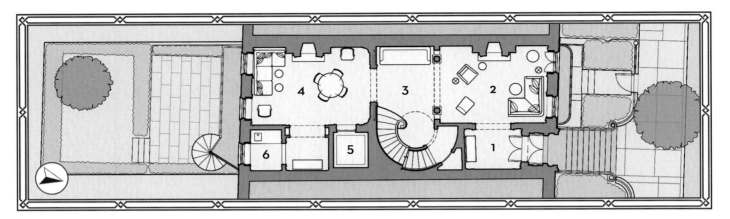

FLOOR PLAN

Following the irregular Greenwich Village lot, the plan is slightly out of square.

1 Entrance Vestibule

2 Front Parlor

3 Stair Hall

4 Rear Parlor

5 Elevator

6 Service Pantry

spirals up the full six floors of the house. More compact, this solution allowed PPA to incorporate larger stair halls on each floor and provide a moment of architectural drama through the core of the house.

Though the clients loved the historic character of their house, they also gravitated toward contemporary art and furniture. A collaboration between PPA and decorator Shawn Henderson, the interiors are chic and rich in texture and interest, incorporating artwork by Cindy Sherman, George Condo, and Matthew Barney, with elaborate millwork and craftsmanship throughout. On the parlor level, freestanding fluted Corinthian columns screen the intermediary stair hall and differentiate it from the front and back rooms. With unusually high ceilings and French windows to the north and south, the floor is open from front to back, and paneled walls, arched doorways, pocket doors, and opulent plaster cornices punctuate the space. PPA restored two of the original carved-marble mantelpieces and incorporated them back into the library on the second floor and the primary bedroom on the fourth floor. Sleek and modern in spirit, the penthouse sunroom and bathroom offer an antidote to the more traditional rooms downstairs, creating a rooftop refuge that overlooks planted terraces and the neighboring rooftops of Greenwich Village.

OPPOSITE
New Corinthian columns divide the front and back parlors. Featuring paneled walls, arched openings, and intricate plaster cornices with cast-plaster ornament, these rooms have the most elaborate millwork and details in the house.

OVERLEAF LEFT
New French windows overlooking the street draw light into the front parlor.

OVERLEAF RIGHT
In the rear parlor, French doors open out to a new areaway and spiral stair that accesses the garden below.

LEFT AND ABOVE
A skylit round stair with a dark walnut handrail spirals up the full six floors of the house.

OPPOSITE
Sleek millwork in the second-floor library, coupled with Shawn Henderson's crisp interior design, reflects PPA's goal to create a classical contemporary house.

One of two intricately carved original marble mantels in the house was restored and reinstalled in the library.

OPPOSITE
Moroccan tiles, circa 1950 French holophane ceiling lights, and a honed Absolute Black granite bolection mantel bring a new style to the kitchen of this nineteenth-century house.

ABOVE
PPA designed a custom stainless-steel range hood for the kitchen, which is appointed with white cabinetry and black granite countertops. French doors open out to the garden.

THE BENSON

P PA was commissioned as design architect by the Naftali Group for this eighteen-story, 75,000-square-foot building at 1045 Madison Avenue, a prominent site between 79th and 80th Streets that is adjacent to Kenneth Murchison's 1925 building, which is crowned by Emily Post's former penthouse duplex. Overlooking a full city block of turn-of-the-century townhouses and an open areaway to the south, The Benson rises almost as a freestanding tower, capturing the energy and elegance of New York's celebrated Art Deco apartment houses of the late 1920s.

Taking its cues from such neighboring Upper East Side landmarks as the Carlyle and Mark hotels, PPA's design also draws inspiration from the surrounding apartment houses of McKim, Mead & White, Rosario Candela, and Emery Roth. It is well grounded in tradition but embraces the Jazz Age ebullience embodied by the work of such celebrated architects as Ely Jacques Kahn, Ralph T. Walker, and Shreve, Lamb & Harmon. The main entrance, set between retail spaces, is delineated as a three-bay section that conveys the intimacy of a townhouse. The hand-carved, hand-laid Indiana limestone façade is enhanced by custom lanterns, an entrance canopy, and bespoke metal grilles inspired by the work of French metal artist Edgar Brandt. As the building ascends, fluted spandrels and chamfered corners that spread softly upward in stepped forms create a sculptural energy; molded parapets and great stylized urns mark the setbacks. Multi-light windows in the main symmetrical block of the building allow for bright, well-lit interiors; in the set-back southern section, a vertical strip of metal-paneled bay windows varies the fenestration pattern. Traditional cast-iron railings—some wrought with a circle-and-star pattern—and iron planters above the

entrance, reminiscent of the Plaza Athénée in Paris, add interest and texture. At the top, PPA treated the mechanical tower like a soaring pavilion with a collocal, blind serliana facing the avenue, and the striking vertical folds of the façade lend a distinctive flair to the streetscape.

At street level, PPA incorporated three retail spaces, designing the finishes for a store of the Milan-based Italian clothier Davide Cenci. The lower floors contain a studio, two two-bedrooms, and a large garden duplex with a sizable rear terrace, as well as a wood-paneled residents' lounge and a garden terrace on the second floor at the rear of the building. In addition to the various amenity spaces—fitness center, multipurpose room, screening room, and art space—PPA laid out sixteen units of simplexes and duplexes. Eleven full-floor suites comprise the bulk of the building, with terraces incorporated into the setbacks as the building rises and recedes. Crowning the top floors are two magnificent duplexes with high ceilings, elegantly curved stairs, and myriad terraces that take advantage of the views of Central Park to the west and the cityscape to the south.

Within the apartments—most endowed with three exposures—PPA strung the public rooms along Madison Avenue and located the primary suite in the southern bay and the secondary bedrooms in the rear. While the proportions, details, and plans of each unit are assured and timeless, PPA's pared-down architectural details, oversized windows, French doors, and generous ceiling heights create a bright simplicity more in tune with

ABOVE LEFT
The chamfered corners of the setbacks and fluted spandrels add texture to the façade.

ABOVE RIGHT
In a nocturnal view, the limestone glows in the reflected light of New York City. Rendering by Coltan Severson.

contemporary living. From the elevator vestibule, glass entry doors with custom metal grilles open onto a barrel-vaulted entrance hall, beyond which extends an elegant enfilade of rooms—library, living room, and dining room—each with chevron-patterned oak floors. Details such as the sleek Pietra Gray marble mantel in the living room, hand-carved Nero Marquina marble vanity in the powder room, and custom hardware by Lowe give each apartment a bespoke quality. Pocket doors separate the dining room from the kitchen, designed in collaboration with cabinetmaker Christopher Peacock and featuring PPA's signature backlit fluted-glass-and-nickel range hood and Calacatta Gold marble countertops. Airy, sun-filled rooms, underscored by a rich but neutral palette of materials, reflect the modern-day interpretation of the classic New York mansion in the sky. From the elegant façades to the fine details of the interiors, PPA wove the lessons learned from working within New York's pedigreed addresses into this impressive new edifice.

In 2022, the Institute of Classical Architecture & Art honored The Benson with a McKim, Mead & White Award for excellence in the classical tradition of a multi-unit project in residential architecture.

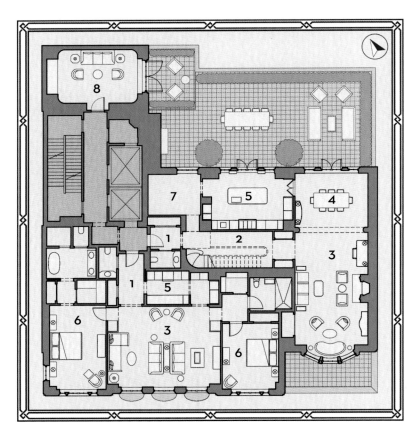

2ND-FLOOR PLAN

The lower floor of a large garden duplex and a wood-paneled residents' lounge and garden terrace to the rear occupy the second floor.

1 Entrance Vestibule	4 Dining Room	7 Library
2 Stair Hall	5 Kitchen	8 Residents' Lounge
3 Living Room	6 Bedroom	

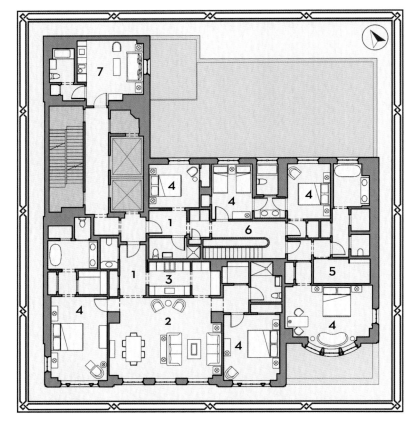

3RD-FLOOR PLAN

A two-bedroom apartment and the upper level of the duplex comprise the third floor.

1 Entrance Vestibule	4 Bedroom	6 Stair Hall
2 Living Room	5 Dressing Room	7 Studio
3 Kitchen		

RIGHT
The intimate three-bay entrance to the apartment building features custom lanterns, an entrance canopy, and metal grilles inspired by the work of French metal artist Edgar Brandt.

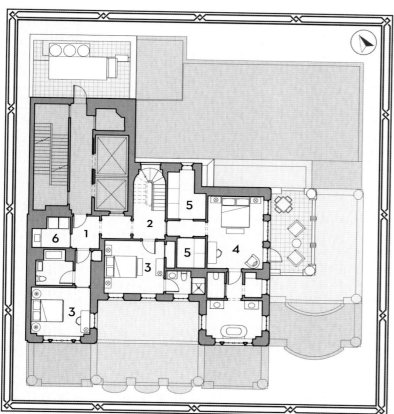

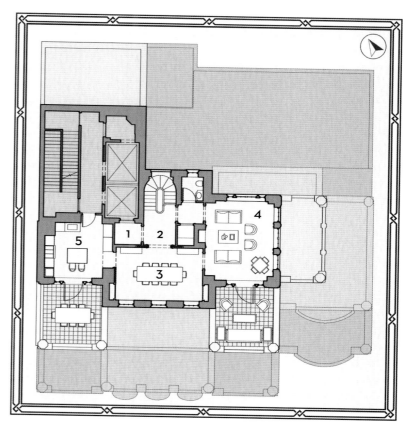

18TH-FLOOR PLAN

In the uppermost duplex, the bedroom level is set below the entertaining floor, accessed by a great sweeping stair.

1 Entrance Vestibule 3 Bedroom 5 Dressing Room
2 Stair Hall 4 Primary Bedroom 6 Laundry Room

19TH-FLOOR PLAN

The public level is centered on a large dining room and features two terraces to take in the views.

1 Entrance Vestibule 3 Dining Room 5 Kitchen
2 Stair Hall 4 Living Room

151 EAST 78TH STREET

For this project, PPA applied its decades of knowledge working within New York buildings designed by such masters as J. E. R. Carpenter, Rosario Candela, and Emery Roth. A new seventeen-story, 66,000-square-foot red-brick and limestone apartment building, developed by Spruce Capital Partners, it was constructed from the ground up. Located just outside the Upper East Side Historic District, it sits between a 1900s tenement to the west and a group of landmarked brick Italianate rowhouses built in 1861 to the east. A well-traveled side street with a variety of building types, 78th Street also features brownstones and brick townhouses from the 1890s, tenements, and the Morgan Studios, a pair of Art Deco apartment buildings from 1928.

Acknowledging the scale and character of the neighborhood, PPA incorporated many of the devices used by the city's early twentieth-century apartment-house designers to anchor the building within its context. At street level, a two-story rusticated limestone base relates in scale to the low-lying rowhouses next door. An arched window above the bronze-and-glass front doors calls out the main entrance, which PPA enhanced with a scrolling split pediment. Above, a carved keystone reinforces the symmetry of the façade and marks the shift between the stone base and the red-brick shaft, which PPA modulated with limestone spandrels that accentuate the verticality of the banks of windows. Traditional cast-iron balconies with decorative anthemion railings add texture and ornament, relieving the mass of the midsection, and multi-light, double-hung windows, typical of prewar apartment houses, relate to the domestic scale of the street. Following the example of Rosario Candela, who, in response to setback rules, often articulated the top floors of his buildings as a series of cascading terraces, PPA offset the penthouse levels and terraces to evoke more romantic forms. At the thirteenth floor, the façade

swoops up to envelop a west-facing limestone bay, a detail that PPA also incorporated on the seventeenth floor to soften the rectilinear lines of the building. Adorning the top floor is a series of limestone-accented oculi, reminiscent of Delano & Aldrich's bull's-eye windows in the design of the attic story of such buildings as the Willard Straight house on Fifth Avenue and 1040 Park Avenue. To enliven the skyplane, PPA introduced a series of limestone urns, each over six feet tall—a dramatic flourish frequently used by New York firm Warren & Wetmore in the 1910s and 1920s in place of a traditional projecting cornice to reinforce the building's presence in the sky.

Though the 57-foot-wide lot provided space for gracious layouts, building requirements, including fire stairs and elevators, as well as various zoning regulations, made the planning challenging. At its deepest, the footprint stretches back 82 feet, but most of the building is 62 feet deep. Because the code limited windows on the east and west sides, PPA designed a contrasting brick pattern to enliven these flat elevations. The building includes fourteen three- to six-bedroom floor-through units. On the lower floors (3–11), the typical plan consists of an enfilade of rooms—the library, living room, and dining room—that spans the south-facing front of the building. Each of these rooms opens onto the next through a set of pocket doors. A long, barrel-vaulted gallery with marble details connects the public spaces and kitchen to the rear, north-facing wing, where PPA incorporated four bedrooms and bathrooms. PPA also used pocket doors to separate the kitchen and dining room, enabling light to filter back into the apartment. Below, on the first and second floors, a maisonette features, in addition to the standard layout, an entry hall, stair, den, and garden in the back courtyard at the lobby level.

As the building begins to set back above the eleventh floor, the apartments become more individualized, featuring duplex layouts, curved stairs, bays, and terraces. The duplex on the twelfth and thirteenth floors has a south- and west-facing terrace, a large living room, and five bedrooms on the upper level, with a rounded, west-facing bay in the primary suite. Above a smaller simplex on the fourteenth floor, PPA designed a five-bedroom, 7,000-square-foot duplex. Here, the elevator hall opens onto a long, sunlit gallery that connects to a stair that ascends through both floors to a third level, where a hallway lit by oculi leads to an expansive, private rooftop terrace.

PRECEDING PAGES
PPA incorporated many devices of early twentieth-century apartment design into the building, including the decorative ironwork and the granite and rusticated limestone of its two-story base, which conforms to the scale of the streetscape.

OPPOSITE
PPA lined the lobby's walls with nailhead-studded brown leather panels and appointed it with Art Deco–inspired furniture.

ABOVE LEFT
The top floors of the building, set back in accord with zoning regulations, are embellished with limestone-accented oculi and limestone urns.

ABOVE RIGHT
Bronze glazed doors, capped by a scrolling split pediment, arched window, and keystone, announce the main entrance to the building.

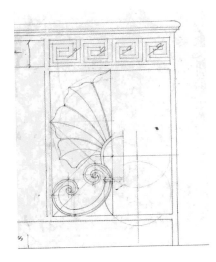

FAR LEFT
The solid buff Indiana limestone urns embellishing the roofline are more than six feet tall. They were turned and then hand carved by the Bybee Stone Company, which is now run by the third generation of the Bybee family.

LEFT
A study for the ironwork of the terrace railings. Drawing by Gregory Gilmartin.

BELOW LEFT
The setback above the eleventh floor creates a west-facing window bay that overlooks a terrace.

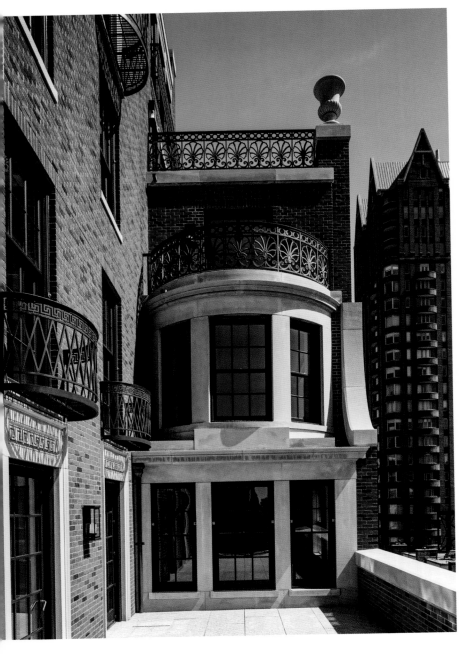

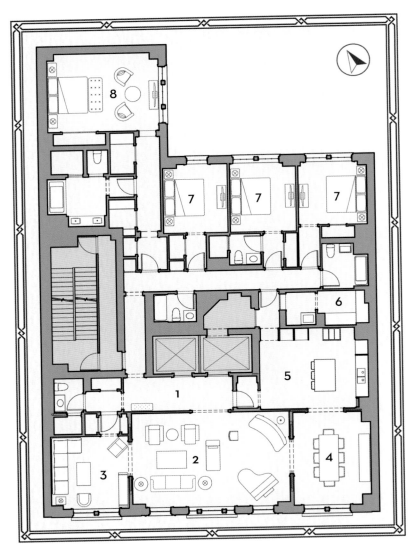

TYPICAL FLOOR PLAN

On the 3rd–11th floors, the public rooms align along the south-facing front of the building; four bedrooms are located in the rear, facing north.

1 Gallery
2 Living Room
3 Library
4 Dining Room
5 Kitchen
6 Laundry Room
7 Bedroom
8 Primary Bedroom

Before construction began, PPA opened a sales gallery on Madison Avenue that included model interiors to convey the scale of the apartments and the integrity of the finishes, as well as a highly detailed 1/50-scale model of the building. PPA designed the marble-clad kitchens with custom range hoods and lighting and the bathrooms with custom vanities, all in a light palette of stone, tile, and millwork. PPA also designed the building's public spaces—the lobby, basement fitness room, residents' library, and garden. In the library, French doors open out to a courtyard centered on a black granite fountain. Warm and club-like, the intimate lobby is clad in a grid of brown leather panels studded with nailheads and furnished with Art Deco–inspired furnishings and custom-made sconces. In 2016, 151 East 78th Street received a Stanford White Award, recognizing excellence in the classical tradition, from the Institute of Classical Architecture & Art.

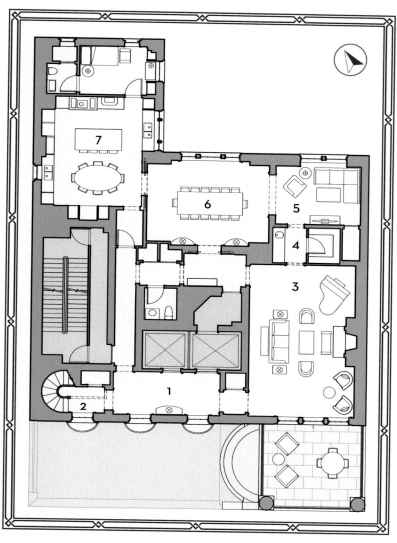

15TH-FLOOR PLAN

On the lower floor of the penthouse duplex, a small terrace opens off the living room; the kitchen, dining room, and library are in the rear.

1 Gallery
2 Stair Hall
3 Living Room
4 Bar
5 Library
6 Dining Room
7 Kitchen

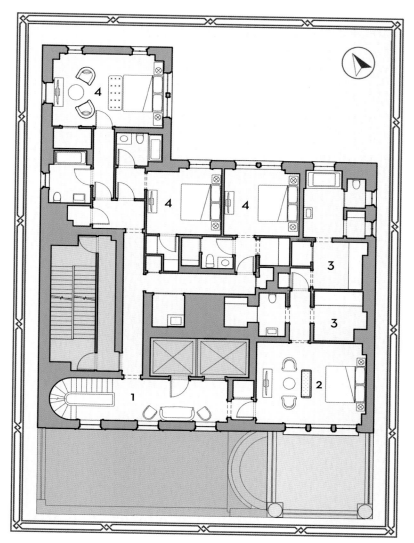

16TH-FLOOR PLAN

A curved stair leads to the bedroom level and up to the private terrace on the roof of the building.

1 Gallery
2 Primary Bedroom
3 Dressing Room
4 Bedroom

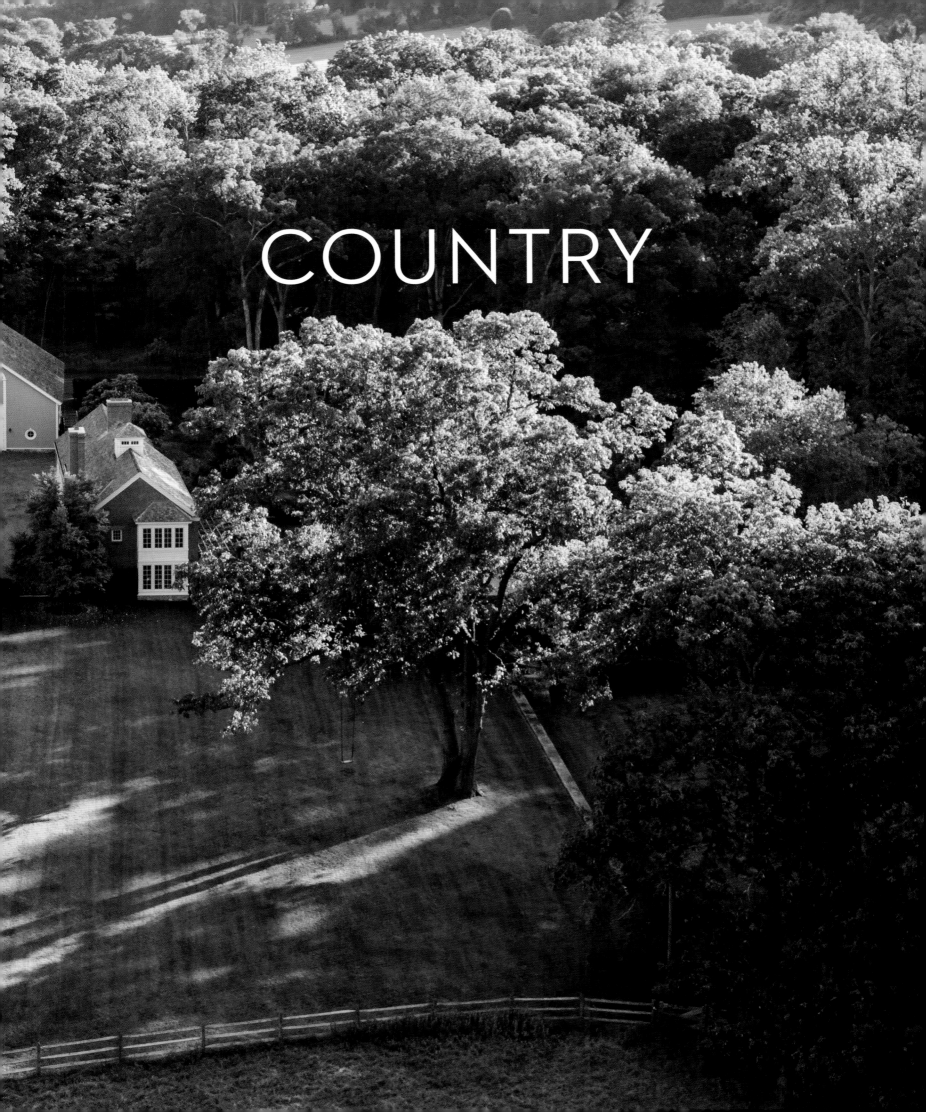

COUNTRY

ARTS AND CRAFTS HOUSE IN OHIO

A bucolic landscape of rolling ridges, dense maple forests, fields, pastures, rivers, and brooks, the Chagrin River Valley is one of the loveliest spots in northeastern Ohio. Part of the Lake Erie watershed just outside Cleveland—once one of the country's major manufacturing hubs—the region had been a summer colony for the city's newly affluent during its boomtown years. Gradually, it evolved into a year-round community, with historic farmhouses and manors nestled in its beautiful and varied countryside. There, on a twenty-nine-acre estate carved out of dense forest, PPA designed a new 14,000-square-foot Arts and Crafts–style house for the owners, a young family ready to put down roots.

For the exterior of the house, the clients let PPA take the lead. Familiar with the area's architectural traditions, PPA turned to the work of Harrie T. Lindeberg and his British counterparts C. F. A. Voysey and Sir Edwin Lutyens, virtuosos at weaving together the irregular threads of the romantic and vernacular with the more rigorous and logical elements of the classical idiom. So inspired, PPA designed a whitewashed-brick-and-limestone Arts and Crafts house that elegantly incorporates picturesque elements such as dormer windows, rambling side wings, and curved bays into a balanced, overall symmetrical composition. PPA reinforced the symmetry of the primary south and north elevations with center doors, substantial copper-capped chimneys, a hipped roof, and pairs of gables, as well as a porte cochere supported by pairs of limestone Doric columns at the entrance and colossal window bays trimmed in limestone on the garden façade. As the house spreads to the east and west, its aesthetic language becomes less formal with side porches, lower-scale pavilions, and a quirky jog in the façade that incorporates the curve of a back staircase. The variegated-gray slate roof with russet-colored accents takes on an organic form, its movement reflecting the shapes of the rooms within, expressed by dormers, jogs, hips, and gables. Working with landscape architect Edmund Hollander, PPA set the house on a gentle slope, centered on an existing pond, and planted the grounds with staghorn sumac and inkberry, as well as beds of rhododendron, pachysandra, evergreen azalea, and cotoneaster.

Planning for the next chapters of their lives, the owners gave PPA more direction for the interiors. Having lived in a house with an open-plan layout, they knew they preferred defined rooms. They wanted the primary suite on the first floor, along with the entertaining rooms, and the children's rooms upstairs so that they can be closed off once the kids are grown and leave the house. A close collaboration from the outset with the interior designers, Miles Redd and David Kaihoi of Redd Kaihoi, allowed the décor and PPA's architecture to play off each other to best effect. Known for colorful

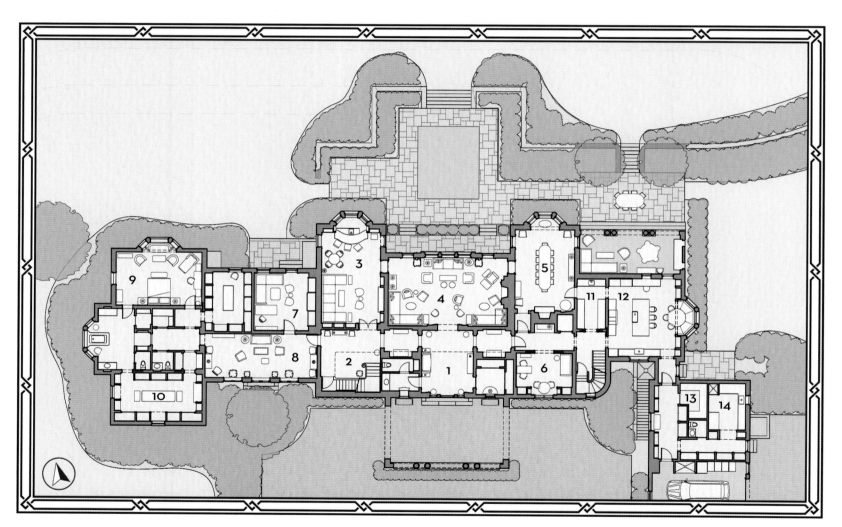

FLOOR PLAN

Though the main block of the house is symmetrical, the layout is more informal to the east and west.

1 Entrance Hall	6 Her Office	11 Butler's Pantry
2 Stair Hall	7 His Study	12 Kitchen
3 Family Room	8 Conservatory	13 Pantry
4 Living Room	9 Primary Bedroom	14 Laundry Room
5 Dining Room	10 Dressing Room	

LEFT
A two-story bay with the kitchen on the lower floor, a steep slate roof with terra-cotta chimney pots, and narrow arched openings set within an infill on the kitchen porch all lend the east wing of the house a picturesque quality.

ABOVE
The entrance to the house is beneath a porte cochere supported by pairs of Doric columns.

and quirky interpretations of old-world glamour, Redd Kaihoi's decoration beautifully complements the voluptuous architectural details of PPA's lofty interiors, giving each room a distinct character.

With classical rigor, the first floor is organized around axes and unfolds in enfilades. The porte cochere opens into a double-height entry hall, its floor laid with Crema Lyon limestone punctuated by squares of Absolute Black granite. The entry hall, in turn, opens into the twenty-foot-high living room with walls that Redd painted an arresting taxicab yellow. Because its colossal window is centered on the front door, the connection to the outdoors and the pond beyond registers from the moment one enters the house. The ample wall space is home to paintings, hangings, mirrors, and urns that Redd positioned to allow breathing room for PPA's scrolling brackets, window enframements, bracketed overdoors, keystones, and pediments. A secondary axis, underscored by a series of graceful arches, opens off the entry hall and runs east–west. It accesses the dining room, elegantly clad in a de Gournay panoramic wallpaper, to the east, and the family room, which features a fanciful canopied bar, to the west. Both rooms overlook the pond. In the stair hall of the east–west axis, a great

RIGHT
The volume of the double-height entry hall invites bold classical details. The Crema Lyon limestone and Absolute Black granite floor is laid in a geometric pattern.

OPPOSITE
An enfilade of arches connects the entry hall and stair hall.

OVERLEAF LEFT
The great window in the double-height living room overlooking the pond is flanked by pedimented doorways and upper windows supported by brackets.

OVERLEAF RIGHT
A bridge-like hall on the second floor with a chinoiserie railing overlooks the twenty-foot-high space; a strigilate plaster frieze above the doorway recalls Renaissance details.

casement window draws sunlight across the curve of the stair and the deep blue chinoiserie railing—a fresh take on an age-old classic. To the east of the dining room, the axis connects to the kitchen wing. The bright white kitchen, featuring a cork tile floor, turquoise accents, and a cozy banquette set into a bay, opens out to a comfortable porch with a seating area, dining area, and an outdoor cooking range. Culminating the axis to the west, a conservatory with wood floors painted to simulate stone is lit by three arched French doors and lined with an Italian panoramic wallpaper. An inviting indoor-outdoor seating area decorated with greenery, it also serves as the entry point for the primary suite, which comprises the bedroom, husband's study, his-and-her dressing rooms, and a chic, blue-painted bathroom with a black-and-white geometrically patterned marble floor and a bathtub extending out from a window bay.

Upstairs, PPA imbued the two wallpapered guest suites, playroom, and pair of children's rooms with character by incorporating bays, window seats, and vestibules; in the bathrooms, showers set into dormers add a bohemian charm. To connect the two sides of the house, PPA designed a bridge-like balcony, also with a blue-painted chinoiserie railing, that overlooks the double-height entry hall to the south and living room to the north, a device that offers different and unexpected vantage points through the interiors to the landscape beyond.

LEFT
The dining room is lined
with a de Gournay panoramic
wallpaper depicting views of
India. A bay window overlooks
the pond.

ABOVE
A blind arch to the left of
a plaster bolection mantel
mirrors the arched doorway
leading to the living room
on the right.

ABOVE
In the kitchen, the simple, white-painted cabinets are enlivened
with turquoise accents and Chippendale-inspired wooden
mullions. An expansive island anchors the room.

OPPOSITE
An east-facing bay encompasses a curved banquette;
the floor is laid in cork tile.

OPPOSITE
A great casement window
bathes the stair hall in natural
light, accentuating the curve
of the stair and its deep blue
chinoiserie railing.

RIGHT
The powder room is tented
in a blue-and-white-striped
fabric.

OPPOSITE
Redd Kaihoi's faux-bamboo trim adds to the chinoiserie style of the dressing room.

RIGHT
The bathtub is set into a west-facing bay.

BELOW
The bathroom features a pair of custom vanities with Grigio Toscana marble tops and a floor laid in a geometric pattern of Grigio Toscana and Nero Marquina marble and Glassos crystallized glass.

ABOVE
Upstairs, a bay in a guest room overlooks the grounds of the property.

OPPOSITE
The bay in the primary bedroom looks out on the pond.

OPPOSITE
Paired Doric columns support
the porch extending off the
kitchen.

ABOVE
A door in the west wall of
the conservatory leads to the
primary suite.

Lit by three arched French doors, the conservatory culminates the axis to the west; with wood floors painted to simulate stone, Redd Kaihoi decorated it to complement the Italian panoramic wallpaper and greenery outside.

NORTH SHORE ESTATE

Astoried property on the North Shore of Massachusetts, this estate was purchased at the turn of the twentieth century by real estate investor George R. White, the president of the Potter Drug & Chemical Company, who promptly tore down the existing farmhouse. In 1898 he commissioned the Boston firm of Winslow & Wetherell to design a shingled house on the site, but by 1913, White's tastes had changed. He brought on Bigelow & Wadsworth—the successor firm to Winslow & Wetherell—to transform his towered seaside cottage into a grand château and Olmsted Brothers to enhance the grounds' park-like quality. Intriguingly, the interim house was not torn down; instead, its walls were encased in imported French tapestry brick and Indiana limestone, which was then carved by top craftsmen brought over from Italy. The interior retained much of its original floor plan, but with its palatial ornament, monumental chimneys, turrets, dormers, finials, and spires, the new exterior of the house, set high on a ridge sloping down toward the water, cut a striking silhouette on the Massachusetts shoreline.

Left vacant in the 1930s and 1940s, the house—a local landmark—was occupied through the subsequent decades without being updated. Its façades still displayed François I detail, but time had taken its toll. The roof, a complex, sculptural form in slate with elaborate copper elements, though enduringly picturesque, had fallen into disrepair. The grand interiors on the main floor, many of which were octagonal or oval-shaped, retained their robust architectural detailing, but later alterations—like a new powder room jammed into the sitting room—had compromised the architecture. The kitchen, a relic of the 1960s, was still located in the basement, and the various bathrooms were a jumble of later interventions. Uninsulated and with antiquated mechanical systems, the house consumed huge amounts of

heating oil to little avail; in the winter, icy condensation coated the windows.

As champions of the property's history, the new owners were enthusiastic about maintaining its architectural integrity, but they wanted to make the house feel inviting and livable. For the interior design, they brought on the British decorator and antiques dealer Max Rollitt to achieve this goal in collaboration with PPA. Rollitt designed the interiors and the furnishings in accordance with the scale and grandeur of the rooms but enlivened them with a modern sensibility. PPA painstakingly restored the original public rooms on the main floor; everything that made the house special was revitalized. Finishes were brought back to life using the least intrusive methods possible; in some cases, surfaces such as the stone carving in the summer room were simply carefully brushed, whereas in rooms with little original fabric, more extensive work was required. On the first floor, the ornate architectural detail—leaded glass, ribbed ceilings, elaborate carving, plasterwork, and flooring—was meticulously restored. Throughout the house and outbuildings, original doors, transoms, and moldings were repurposed to fit modified floor plans. Other areas, like the basement and the third floor, were completely gutted and reframed. The new rooms, surfaces, and details follow the spirit of the house so faithfully that the improvements are difficult to identify. For the renovation of the basement kitchen, for example, PPA clad walls in white glazed ceramic tile and covered the floor in reclaimed limestone; Rollitt chose a mustard-yellow trim to brighten the space. The bedrooms, both existing and reconfigured, were furnished with a mix of antiques and newly commissioned pieces by Rollitt, while PPA modernized the bathrooms in a traditional vein with ceramic tile, wood, marble, white paint, and clawfoot tubs. And of course, PPA maintained the secret passageway—practically a requirement in such a house—a hidden stair leading from the second floor to a third-floor study.

Given the amount of energy needed to heat and cool the 24,000-square-foot house, the clients embraced a more environmentally friendly approach. Rather than incorporating a modern air-conditioning system, PPA renewed and improved the original passive, fan-based ventilation system. Layers of insulation and vapor barriers were inserted within the original walls, and systems were calibrated to achieve an energy-efficient envelope appropriate to the preservation of the house. By installing a network of ventilation ducts and restoring the whole house fan in the attic, PPA enabled the house to take maximum advantage of the prevailing breezes off the ocean in summer; a geothermal system heats the house in winter.

In addition, PPA designed two new outbuildings—a garage with a second-floor apartment and a tennis pavilion—as well as a pool folly. Much like Grosvenor Atterbury's stone barns for John D. Rockefeller Jr. at Pocantico Hills, New York, these structures are carried out in rustic fieldstone to contrast with the more formal house, giving the impression that the property has been developed gradually over time. Materials were carefully selected for their beautiful patina. For example, the barn-like stone garage structure, located behind

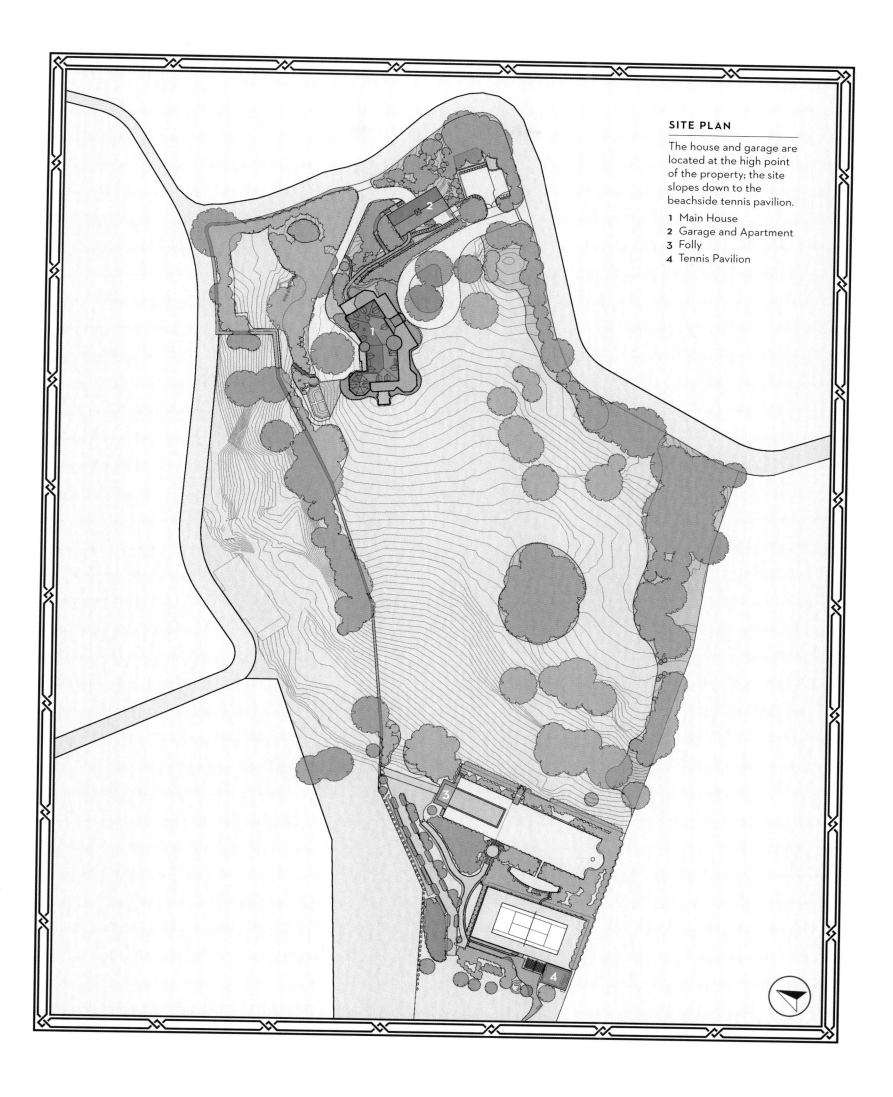

SITE PLAN

The house and garage are located at the high point of the property; the site slopes down to the beachside tennis pavilion.

1 Main House
2 Garage and Apartment
3 Folly
4 Tennis Pavilion

ABOVE LEFT
A fieldstone folly by the pool resembles the ruins of an eighteenth-century iron furnace; its entrance is a rustic wood plank door with wrought-iron strap hinges and a monolithic stone lintel framing the opening.

ABOVE RIGHT
PPA designed the new barn-like fieldstone structure that contains a garage, gym, and apartment. Different in style and material from the main house, it suggests that the estate was developed over time.

CENTER
A study of the stone detail in the tennis pavilion. Rendering by Anton Glikin.

RIGHT
The tennis pavilion's stone details evoke the architecture of the main house.

OPPOSITE
A trellised seating area extends from the fieldstone tennis pavilion overlooking the bay.

the house, incorporates wood and support beams from a late-1700s barn in Delaware and hand-hammered hardware from a 300-year-old forge in Connecticut. A caretaker's apartment, gym, and studio occupy the upper level; the eight-car garage below is accessed through an arched entry, the stone for which was handpicked and hand laid.

Down the gentle slope toward the shoreline, the pool is anchored by a folly that PPA designed to resemble the ruins of an eighteenth-century iron furnace—an early industrial structure typical of New England. Serving as both a retaining wall and a storage room, the formation also features a lounging terrace. Its stone was also handpicked and hand laid. At the base of the property near the beach, the rustic stone beach and tennis pavilion features more polished carved-stone detail—fictional spolia retrieved from a prior structure—that hints at the sophistication of the main house. An arched glass door, echoing the shape of the wooden doors of the garage and pool folly, opens into a kitchenette with a green tile floor, bathrooms, and stairs leading to an upper terrace with an outdoor fireplace. Here, the property can be experienced in its full glory. Over time, the grounds had been reshaped with substantial volumes of imported soil and stone, but Lolly Gibson of Laura Gibson Landscape Design, a landscape architect deeply familiar with the estate's history, returned the grounds to their open, flowing, park-like form. Relying on the plant lists from the Olmsted archives, she removed many non-indigenous plants and shrubs and restored the great lawn's sweep from the landmark house to the beach below.

1ST-FLOOR PLAN

The first floor contains a number of octagonal rooms, evidence of the original Shingle Style house's plan.

1 Entrance Gallery   4 Dining Room   6 Stair Hall   8 Winter Porch
2 Sitting Room   5 Kitchenette   7 Living Room   9 Summer Porch
3 Tea Room

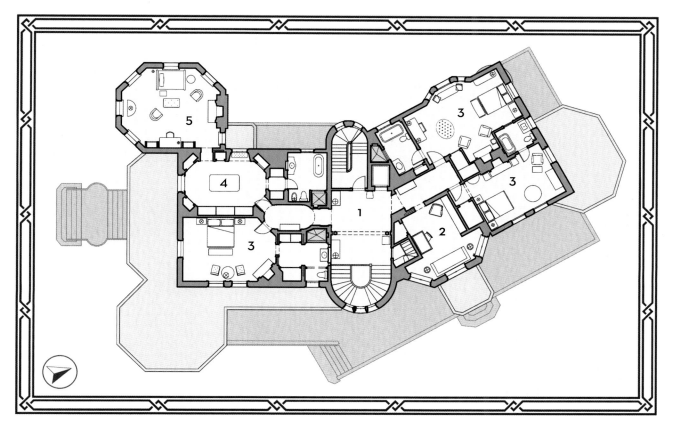

2ND-FLOOR PLAN

The primary suite and guest bedrooms are located on the second floor.

1 Stair Hall   **3** Bedroom   **5** Primary Bedroom

2 Study   **4** Dressing Room

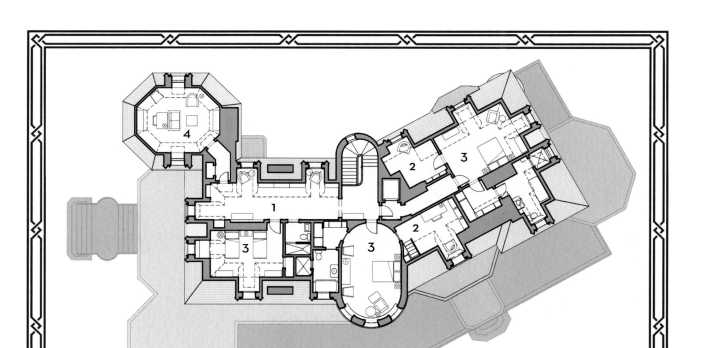

3RD-FLOOR PLAN

The third floor contains the children's rooms, built into the attic eaves.

1 Hall   **2** Study   **3** Bedroom   **4** Office

OPPOSITE
The sanded-limestone walls of the entrance gallery were restored to their original patina. Throughout the first floor, the leaded glass, ribbed ceilings, stone floors, elaborate carvings, plasterwork, woodwork, and wood flooring were all restored.

ABOVE LEFT
The exterior of the heavy walnut front door is carved with details that echo the François I architectural style of the façades.

ABOVE RIGHT
The elaborate historic front door was cleaned, oiled, and hand waxed to bring back its original luster and color.

RIGHT
The restored mosaic floor incorporates both new material and salvaged, restored tiles.

OPPOSITE
The wooden rail and balusters of the main stair were oiled and waxed to restore the wood's patina and rich color.

ABOVE
In the dining room, the elaborate oak carving was cleaned and then treated with tung oil and wax to restore its luster.

ABOVE
The oak paneling and floors in the living room were restored; the knotwork tracery ceiling was first cleaned and then removed to accommodate new plumbing above before being reinstalled.

OPPOSITE
The stucco and limestone in the winter room, soiled by a century of wood fires and cigar smoke, was cleaned by hand brushing.

OPPOSITE

A 1960s powder room that had been haphazardly added was removed to restore the sitting room to its historic shape and appearance.

ABOVE

The original onyx laylight in the tearoom was leaking and cracked. Max Rollitt's interior design, saturated with rich materials, antique treasures, and new furniture designed and made by him, ingeniously captures and embraces the layered history and character of the house.

OPPOSITE
Max Rollitt mixed his own green-blue paint for the cabinets and specified yellow trim for the new basement kitchen. The call bell box, original to the house, was restored to working condition.

ABOVE
PPA found artisans to create new tile for the kitchen walls to match the crackled glazing and age of the originals. The reclaimed-limestone slabs covering the floor were imported from France and laid in a random pattern.

LEFT
A steel embrasure frames the original stove, which was restored to working condition, and the adjacent new European range. On the wall at right, traditional icebox hardware was applied to panels concealing the refrigerators. The marble-topped antique-oak island was designed by Max Rollitt.

ABOVE
The white glazed ceramic tiles in the kitchen emulate the historic bricks in the basement plant room, once the cold storage room, which are original to the house. The terra-cotta floor tiles were existing.

OPPOSITE
The new details of the octagonal basement mudroom, which leads to the kitchen, are in keeping with the spirit of the house.

LEFT
A new bathroom on the second floor, clad in stained walnut paneling and Antique Grey and Paonazzo Grande marble, takes the place of an old closet.

BELOW
PPA designed an octagonal dressing room in the primary suite, reusing salvaged pilasters and moldings to shape the new space. Max Rollitt wrapped the space in a de Gournay chinoiserie wallpaper.

RIGHT
The woodwork in a bedroom on the second floor was completely restored.

ABOVE
On the third floor, existing doors and transoms were removed and reused as the new openings to a bathroom and bedroom.

OPPOSITE
A third-floor bedroom, swathed in Adelphi's Butterfly Chintz wallpaper, is tucked into attic dormers. Blue plaster bead molding outlines the dormers' angles.

LEFT
A new bedroom on the third floor fits into a turret.

ABOVE
The third-floor hallway was gutted and rebuilt in the spirit of a historic New England attic floor with quirky angles and dormers. Flooring was salvaged from other parts of the house.

LONG ISLAND BEACH HOUSE

Set on a flat stretch of farmland with sweeping views of vegetable fields, a tidal pond, and the Atlantic Ocean, this 15,000-square-foot Shingle Style beach house was designed to capitalize on the natural beauty of the surroundings but not to infringe upon them. The shingled vernacular, curved bays, porches, and picturesque dormers evoke the informality of summer resort architecture and form a serene addition to a historic property.

For their year-round residence, the owners asked PPA to design a house large enough to host sizable gatherings and plenty of guests but intimate enough for quiet family weekends. To temper the size and ambitiousness of the program, PPA organized the plan in three narrow masses that angle in on the water side but open out on the rear side of the site. A wreath of narrow porches and piazzas—both screened and open-air—encircles the house, forging an easy connection between indoors and outdoors. The primary section of the house boasts two full stories with twin gables, but the second level of the rest of the house consists of dormered bedrooms tucked under the eaves. At a story and a half, the height falls below the tree line. Simple gables, pulled back from the first-floor roofline, allow for unbroken eaves and balconies to be carved into the roof. The movement created by the different volumes and massing gives the cedar shingle an organic quality. A porte cochere angles obliquely off the southwestern side of the house, concealing four garage doors on the far side.

Though the exterior is accretive, with various jogs and bump-outs that give the elevations a spontaneous character, as if various wings and rooms were added over time, the interiors, decorated by Victoria Hagan in shades of blue and white, are calm and disciplined. Sleek rooms with white walls, deeply stained white oak floors, and high-gloss ceilings flow comfortably

PRECEDING PAGES
An abundance of narrow porches and piazzas encircle the house, forging an easy connection between indoors and outdoors, and simple gables pulled back from the first-floor roofline allow for unbroken eaves and balconies to be carved out of the roof.

from one to the next across the main floor of the house. Only one room deep, the ground-floor plan ensures light and air from both east and west. As an overture, the front entry opens into a skylit, double-height paneled hall with a stately fireplace, reminiscent of the traditional living hall in the great Shingle Style cottages of the 1890s. The space connects to a lofty paneled stair hall with a coffered ceiling and an upper-level window that creates a dialogue between the main stair and the entry hall. A parallel pair of long axes through the main rooms—one from the chestnut-paneled library, through the living room and entry hall, to the stair hall, and the other through the same rooms to the dining room—progress in a series of tall arches. Each room is centered on large, double-hung windows, some of which are grouped in bays that swell onto porches. At the hinge in the plan, the expansive, windowed bay of the dining room curves majestically out to the view; to the south, the bright white kitchen and adjoining family room open onto a screened dining porch.

Upstairs, coved and tray ceilings capture height and volume from space typically left to the attic. PPA centered the barrel-vaulted bedroom hall on a coved vestibule lit by a skylight; many of the secondary bedrooms, including the children's bunk room, are also enhanced by

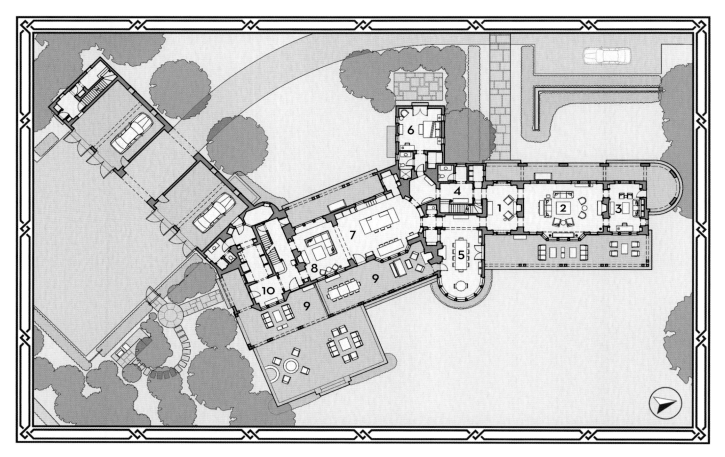

FLOOR PLAN

PPA organized the plan in three narrow masses that are only one room deep, ensuring light and air from both the east and the west.

1 Entrance Hall	5 Dining Room	9 Screened Porch
2 Living Room	6 Bedroom	10 Mudroom
3 Study	7 Kitchen	
4 Stair Hall	8 Family Room	

RIGHT
A rounded bay containing the back stair serves to hinge the main part of the house and the angled garage wing.

FAR RIGHT
A narrow porch with shingled piers announces the front entrance.

BELOW
The shingled vernacular, curved bays, porches, and picturesque dormers evoke the informality of summer resort architecture.

RIGHT
The arched openings in the paneled entry hall frame a fireplace. A laylight in ceiling of the double-height room brings daylight into the core of the house.

OPPOSITE
A series of tall, arched openings mark a parallel pair of long axes that run from the dining room and entrance hall to the living room and library beyond.

coved ceilings. PPA's custom-designed door hardware is used throughout the house, like an elegant signet.

The grounds of the five-acre property, which also includes a historic guesthouse, a tennis pavilion, and a contemporary pool house, have been handsomely designed by Hollander Design Landscape Architects. The farmland landscape beyond is less structured: vegetable and cutting gardens commingle with beehives and chicken coops, and the surrounding fields are planted with clover, daisies, sunflowers, and black-eyed Susans. Beeches, oaks, lindens, and assorted flowering species have been added to the stock of eclectic old-growth trees that embed the new house into its setting.

The crisp. white-painted
moldings give the living room,
lit by a bay of windows, a
simple but tailored presence.

OPPOSITE
The library is paneled in reclaimed bleached American chestnut. A door to the porch beyond is set in an opening in the built-in bookcase.

ABOVE
In the blue butler's pantry, the molding profiles are based on geometries found in Colonial Revival interiors. The dark-stained floors were hand scraped and brought to a glossy sheen, making them appear to have been polished for centuries.

RIGHT
The dining room is lit by six-over-nine double-hung windows arranged in a semicircular bay.

OPPOSITE
The main stair wraps around and over the entry hall vaults, providing a view of the paneled entry hall below.

RIGHT
In the primary suite, a sitting room can be sequestered from the bedroom by pocket doors.

BELOW
The airy primary bedroom has a lofty, twelve-foot-high tray ceiling.

ABOVE LEFT
Shallow wood moldings
form the coffers in the stair
hall ceiling.

ABOVE RIGHT
The curved landing of the
back stair, which features
Chippendale-inspired
balusters, projects into
the rounded bay.

OPPOSITE
One of the children's
bedrooms is outfitted with
bunk beds tucked beneath
the slope of a gable.

SEVENTEENTH-CENTURY GUESTHOUSE

Located on a wide swath of farmland near the ocean, the Osborne-Topping House (ca. 1690) has been moved and altered several times over the course of its history. As one of the oldest extant structures in Suffolk County, Long Island, both the owner and PPA recognized the importance of meticulously restoring the landmark dwelling as part of its transformation into a guest cottage for an adjoining property. Originally a four-bay saltbox, the house was expanded in stages into a five-bay, center-door Colonial with a full second floor by 1750. Though the introduction of two-over-two sashes in the late Victorian era and an unsympathetic single-story kitchen wing in the mid-twentieth century compromised its architectural integrity, the bones of the house were entirely intact. Inside, a near-complete timber frame and a mortise-and-tenon-joined stair, as well as delicate Federal-style recessed paneling, vertical and horizonal wall boards, hardware, stair railing with slender tapered balusters, and floorboards had all survived over the centuries. The rooms were authentic examples of period carpentry and building techniques.

In addition to restoring the house, PPA's brief included connecting it to a nearby early twentieth-century carriage house on the property that also had its original wood frame. An exercise in historic preservation, PPA protected, surveyed, and documented the guesthouse structure before design work began. After the interiors were dismantled, the original elements were stowed for reuse in climate-controlled storage. The house was lifted and carefully moved aside so a new concrete foundation could be laid, at which point thirty inches of rot were removed from the lowest reaches of the white-painted shingled façades. During the design phase, PPA and the client—with the input of the preservation specialist Zach Studenroth—decided to remove the twentieth-century addition and return the house to its latest Colonial-era

PRECEDING PAGES

In restoring one of Suffolk County's oldest structures, PPA used traditional wood shingles, reflecting mid-eighteenth-century building practices, and designed a new batten door and overhang inspired by a neighboring house of the same period. The sage-green paint for the window frames and door is historically based.

RIGHT

French doors flanked by sliding barn doors access an exercise studio, repurposing an early twentieth-century carriage house on the property and salvaging its original timber framing.

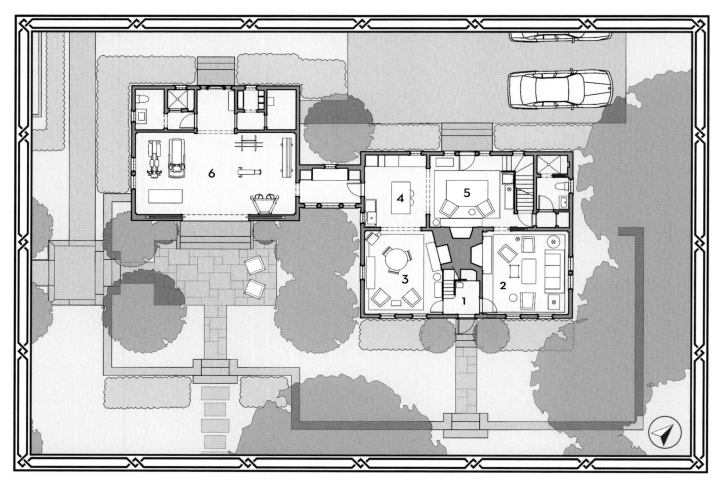

FLOOR PLAN

From the kitchen, a windowed hyphen connects to the exercise studio. In the historic section, three fireplace flues nest in the large central chimney.

1 Entrance Hall   3 Dining Room   5 Family Room
2 Living Room   4 Kitchen   6 Exercise Studio

LEFT
In the family room, a new
back stair was constructed
by studying historic details
and using materials that were
consistent with the original
construction means and
methods.

state and orientation. In place of a Colonial Revival Doric portico that had been added in the mid-1900s, PPA designed a new batten entry door and a simplified overhang inspired by the nearby Thomas Osborne House, a similar dwelling from the same period, the details of which had been documented in the 1940s by the Historic American Buildings Survey.

After the foundation was completed, the house was returned to its original location and its components were pieced back together. The chimney, which had been removed when the house was moved, was rebuilt with handmade bricks, and the façades and roof were sheathed in traditional wood shingle, reflecting mid-eighteenth-century building practices. Also in keeping with the Colonial period, PPA's design reintroduced twelve-over-twelve windows crafted by specialists to match details of the John Howard Payne House, ca. 1720, in East Hampton. In reinforcing the wood frame, PPA took care to preserve the original joints and gunstock posts and to reinstall the interiors using traditional methods and joinery. Missing boards and paneling were replaced with handmade replicas, and new materials—such as the lime-based plaster on the lath walls—were consistent with historical precedents. In the bathrooms, PPA installed free-standing plumbing that did not disturb the original fabric of the house.

As a result, the interiors feel bright and refreshed but authentic and atmospheric. Designer Robert Stilin's warm and inviting decoration enhances the cozy and historic nature of the rooms. Throughout, the white-painted walls highlight the age-worn wood beams—remnants of the late seventeenth-century framing—as well as the floor planks and wall paneling. The cheerful kitchen, clad in glossy, variegated-white tile, connects to the carriage house, which PPA transformed into a gym, its original wood frame salvaged and exposed in its new iteration. Sliding barn doors flank French windows and doors, which draw light into the exercise studio and open it up to views of the immediate landscape, designed by Edmund Hollander, and the water beyond.

In the cozy front living room, the white-painted walls highlight the original wood framing. Nearly every ceiling joist in the original house was saved. Marks were found on the sides of each joist indicating where the plaster ceilings had been located. These were used to set new plaster, which was applied on traditional lath.

COUNTRY

ABOVE
The delicate Federal-style recessed paneling was salvaged and reinstalled in the dining room.

RIGHT
In the kitchen, new glossy variegated-white tile on the walls and marble countertops join the salvaged wood beams of the ceiling and historic floor planks.

OPPOSITE
In the front stair hall, the vertical and horizonal wall boards, floorboards, and slender, tapered balusters of the stair railing were all restored and reinstalled.

ABOVE
An upstairs bedroom with salvaged ceiling beams illustrates the compact domestic scale of seventeenth-century dwellings.

NEW VILLA ON A HISTORIC LONG ISLAND ESTATE

PPA drew inspiration for this new house, located on the grounds of a historic estate in eastern Long Island, from the Mediterranean-style villa that has anchored the twelve-acre property since 1912. Designed by Beaux-Arts-trained architect Grenville T. Snelling, the main house, known as Minden, has been well maintained past its centennial. The architectural language of this local landmark—creamy stucco walls, red-tile roof and overhangs supported by deep muscular brackets, and patterned, wrought-iron railings—provided PPA with a template for the design of this 8,000-square-foot "carriage house," which replaces a derelict garage and staff quarters, for the owner's family.

Although the new house shares Minden's park-like back lawn, pool, and tennis court, PPA established it as a separate residence by giving it its own approach. Governed by an overall symmetry, the north-facing entrance façade is anchored by a two-story pavilion with tall, narrow windows that protrudes slightly from the plane of the house. In the rear, PPA centered the façade on a rounded bay that reaches out into the garden; it is flanked by rectilinear bays with tiled overhangs. The architectural details, including the rafter tails and eaves, roof pitch, trim, shutter cut-outs, balcony railings, and windows, were all inspired by the main house but carried out with a sparer touch. For the new roof, PPA salvaged most of the red slate from the preexisting carriage house and chose the same Donald Kaufman–specified colors for the exterior as those used for the historic mansion.

The intricate, wood-paneled rooms of the main villa were, as described by one periodical of the time, "splendid in [their] spaciousness and simple dignity." Taking this description as a playful challenge, Katie Ridder Interiors gave the new house splendidly bright and fresh interiors, full of vibrant color, lively patterns, an exuberant mix of furnishings, and contemporary art, including Andy Warhol's *Endangered Species*, a collection of ten prints from 1983. PPA organized the public rooms downstairs in a flowing plan anchored by the living room. The centerpiece of the house, it features a large, bowed bay facing the garden and is exotically decorated with a stunning Iznik-patterned wallpaper by Iksel Decorative Arts, as well as with a hand-carved jali screen by Turquoise Mountain in Kabul, Afghanistan, which frames the fireplace. The family room, paneled in cerused white oak, and kitchen flank the living room to the east and west and also overlook the garden. The stained white oak that PPA used for the cabinetry and center island in the kitchen lends it a tailored, furniture-like feel; its bright, windowed bay creates the perfect spot for a table and banquette. At the front of the house, the wood floor in the vivid yellow dining room is painted in a design based on a Moroccan checkerboard pattern. Though the rooms are all

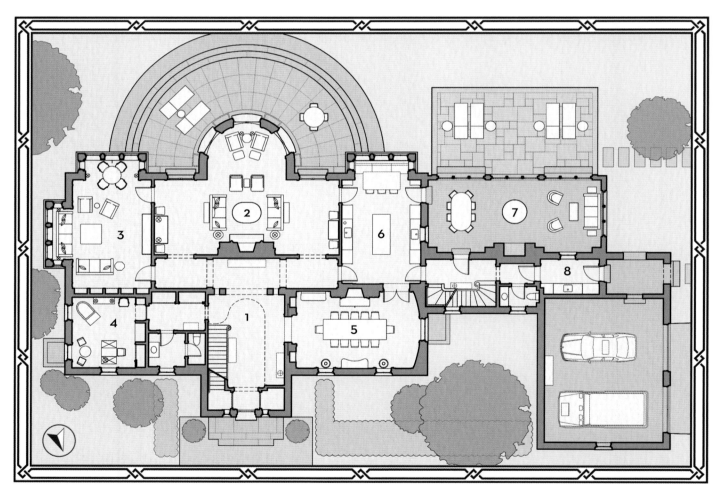

FLOOR PLAN

The main block of the house is symmetrical with a rounded bay that reaches out to the landscape.

1 Entrance Hall
2 Living Room
3 Family Room
4 Office
5 Dining Room
6 Kitchen
7 Screened Porch
8 Mud Room

aligned and interrelated, PPA gives each a distinct character, with varying moldings, wall paneling, materials, and ceiling treatments.

In the dramatic two-story entry hall, the wide switchback stair and gracious curve of the landing and balustrade above are offset by the deep green, glossy Moroccan tile floor and light-colored walls; pairs of Doric piers screen the hallway beyond, which connects the family room, living room, and kitchen/garage wing, tempering the difference in scale between the two spaces. Upstairs, PPA included four comfortable bedroom suites. Directly above the living room, the primary bedroom is lit by a great curved bay of windows, accentuated by rounded ceiling moldings. It connects to a vaulted bathroom with a floor of rich purple Moroccan tile. Oriented to the south, these rooms overlook an allée of trees, designed by landscape architecture firm LaGuardia Design Group, that separates the rear lawn of the house from that of the main house, where a Maya Lin earth sculpture has pride of place.

OPPOSITE
A sweeping switchback stair ascends to a landing that perches over the double-height entrance hall with its dazzling Moroccan tile floor.

ABOVE
The fireplace wall is the focal point of the living room: a walnut, mirror-backed jali screen, hand carved by Turquoise Mountain in Afghanistan, frames a bolection mantel with a surround of Moroccan zellige tile in shades of turquoise.

OVERLEAF
The exuberant Topkapi-inspired wallpaper by Iksel Decorative Arts in the living room blends with the greenery outside, drawn inside through the rounded bay of French doors.

OPPOSITE
The dining room floors are painted in a design based on a Moroccan checkerboard pattern. The black stone bolection mantel creates a striking contrast to Katie Ridder's brightly lacquered walls.

ABOVE
The oak pocket doors connecting the dining room to the entrance hall are flanked by arched glazed niches.

ABOVE
The cerused, rift-sawn white oak cabinetry and island give the kitchen a tailored, furniture-like feel.

OPPOSITE
In the family room, PPA also used cerused, rift-sawn white oak to give the spaces a unified feeling.

ABOVE LEFT
A bull's-eye window in the dressing room echoes the curved profile of the elliptical barrel-vaulted ceiling in the primary bath.

ABOVE RIGHT
The vaulted bathroom is anchored by amethyst Moroccan tiles.

OPPOSITE
The curve of the tray ceiling in the primary bedroom follows the curve of the extra-voluminous window bay.

HOUSE ON GEORGICA POND

On the south shore of Long Island, where generations-old summer houses rarely change hands, there is a quaint, quiet lagoon called Georgica Pond that is renowned for its unspoiled beauty. Set on the edge of one of its idyllic coves, an old summer house charmed its new owners, who could not resist the appeal of the various quirky additions that had been made over the years. Having worked with PPA on a previous project, the owners initially asked Pennoyer and his team to restore the old house, but it was beyond repair: the pipes leaked, the wiring was in bad shape, and the chimneys leaned perilously and would not have survived being raised up six feet as required by FEMA. Though reluctant to build anew in this tradition-bound community, the clients acquiesced, requesting only that the new design preserve the spirit of the old house and the idiosyncratic traits that gave it such allure.

PPA showed the owners the upsides to designing a new house: the old dwelling, though charming, felt dark and closed off and was not winterized. For the new L-shaped, 10,000-square-foot Shingle Style house, PPA set out to evoke a simple beach cottage that had been expanded over generations. Like its predecessor, the house rambles enchantingly, its roofline unfolding in a series of gables and dormers. Re-creating some of the architectural quirks that had given the old house its character, PPA's design includes a similar low, flat-roofed porch supported by piers that angles out to views of the dunes and ocean. On the first floor, every room accesses the outdoors—the pool area, screened and open-air porches, and the beach—forging a strong connection between the interiors and the scenic surroundings. On the façade of the two-story bay fronting the living room and primary bedroom, PPA inserted bronze spandrels carved with the face of a sea goddess—a whimsical touch.

In addition to creating easy outdoor access, the L-shaped plan allowed PPA to designate discrete sections of the house for family and guests. Reflecting the plan of a traditional late nineteenth-century Shingle Style house, the interiors are open and informal, with the stair hall and dining room connected by a wide opening to the entry hall. Though the rooms flow organically from one to the next, they are logically laid out along two intersecting axes. The east–west axis runs from the front porch and door through a set of double French

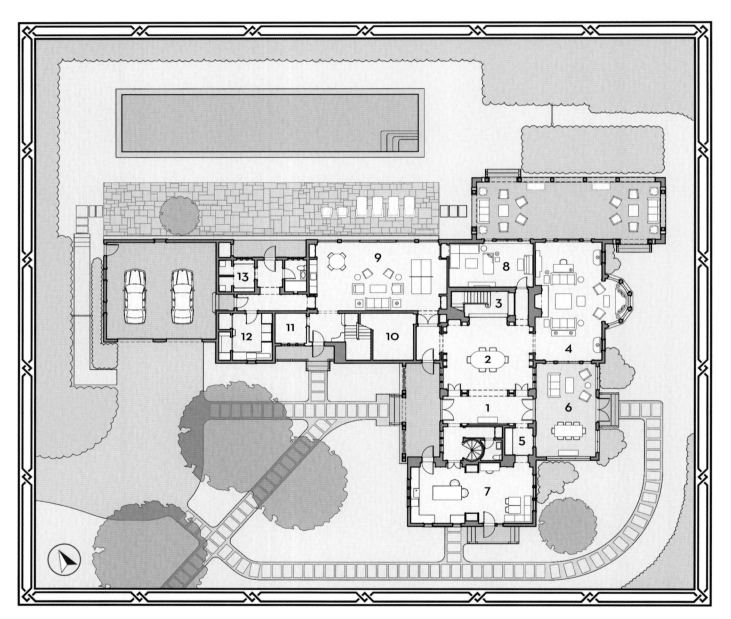

FLOOR PLAN

The front door leads into the public rooms, while a side door accesses the family room and guest wing upstairs.

1 Entrance Hall	6 Screened Porch	11 Coat Closet
2 Dining Room	7 Kitchen	12 Laundry Room
3 Stair Hall	8 TV room	13 Changing Room
4 Living Room	9 Family Room	
5 Pantry	10 Mechanical Room	

doors on the opposite side of the entry hall and out to the screened porch. Along the north–south axis, a series of doors connects the intimate TV room, main stair, dining room, entry hall, pantry, and kitchen. Guests are given a measure of privacy; their accommodations—four bedroom suites tucked into dormers—are accessible through a side porch that leads to the family room and side stair. A whimsical spiral stair inserted between the kitchen, entry hall, and powder room curls up to the family bedroom section. Laylights over both the main and spiral stairs allow daylight to permeate the depth of the house. Throughout, niches, alcoves, and Moorish lattice panels, reminiscent of those that Stanford White incorporated into his Shingle Style summer houses, lend the interiors a winsome quality. Classic, white-painted tongue-and-groove woodwork enhances the feeling of casual beachside living. Adding to the accretive effect are sliding doors in the family room overlooking the pool, evoking the 1950s. For the decoration, Matthew Patrick Smyth opted for patterned prints and colors that create warmth during the bleaker winter months yet enhance the light and breezes of summer; a mix of informal beachy furniture and more exotic finds and antiques lends a layered, long-lived-in look to the house.

The house sits comfortably within the four-acre property's natural surroundings, regenerated by landscape designer Edwina von Gal. Over the years, invasive plant species had overtaken the property. By restoring what was originally there—a mix of bayberry, eastern red cedar, and other hardy trees—von Gal has re-created an enchanting, exuberant landscape that embraces the house as if it has always been there.

TOP LEFT AND RIGHT
Bronze spandrels carved with the face of a sea goddess grace the two-story bay on the gable end of the house. Rendering by Anton Glikin.

ABOVE
A clear axis extends through the house from the front door to a view of the dunes and ocean beyond.

ABOVE
A bay of windows in the living room draws in the views.

RIGHT
The interiors are open, informal, and bright, with lots of doors leading to exterior spaces; in the living room, French doors open out to a porch.

OPPOSITE
Classic, white-painted beadboard in the kitchen enhances the feeling of easy beachside living.

RIGHT
PPA re-created a low, flat-roofed porch with piers angling out to the view, a quirky element of the old house on the site.

BELOW
The white-painted kitchen is centered on an open-base island and features teak floors, black granite countertops, and a PPA-designed range hood.

ABOVE AND RIGHT
The stair hall is flooded with light from a skylight above and features a built-in bench topped by a Moroccan mosharabi screen. The configuration of the combined stair hall, dining room, and entry hall harks back to the great hall of a traditional late nineteenth-century Shingle Style house.

LEFT
The bay of windows in the primary bedroom creates a quiet spot to take in the views.

BELOW
The primary bedroom features an arched, beadboard-paneled niche for reading, one of the quirky elements that gives the interiors character.

ABOVE LEFT
A nautically inspired spiral staircase with portholes looking into the children's rooms leads from the family bedrooms to the public areas below.

ABOVE RIGHT
A bull's-eye window and laylight above the main stair allow light to reach the depth of the house.

ISOLA BELLA

Among the 4,500 islands that hug Maine's craggy coastline, there is one on Penobscot Bay that has been transformed into a lush summer playground—not once, but twice. In the 1890s, William H. Folwell, the proprietor of a successful woolen mill in Philadelphia, cleared the densely wooded, thirty-one-acre island for an Italianate mansion, cottages, docks, swimming pool, tennis court, and music room—all inspired by a trip to the palace and terraced gardens of Isola Bella, one of the Borromean Islands in Lake Maggiore, Italy. In the 1960s, the main house burned, and a smaller cottage was built in its place; on PPA's first site visit, terra-cotta shards of the original mansion's massive Ionic capitals still lay scattered about. PPA chose that same spot, high on a granite bluff, for a new Shingle Style house. In accord with the architectural legacy of the Maine coast, PPA kept the exterior materials—especially on the elevation visible from the water—relatively simple. The façades and gables are wrapped in a dark shingle accented with green trim that blends in with the surrounding conifers. In Maine, where houses are experienced by water as much as by land, its weathered silhouette melds into the coastline, inconspicuous to the passing sailor. To allow light and breezes to pass to and from the land and sea sides, PPA designed a shallow, one-room-deep plan and oriented the main wing, housing the public rooms and primary suite, to the southwest, affording sweeping views of the Camden Hills. Following the hinges and bends of the topography of the island, the kitchen and guest wing veers off at an angle from the main wing at the main stair hall. A complex series of rounded towers, porches, dormers, and jerkinhead gables punctuates the roofline. But, like the early Shingle Style houses of McKim, Mead & White, the intricacy of the massing is tempered by the restrained palette of the cedar shingles—both cut and fish-scale—and painted trim.

PRECEDING PAGES
This new house on a thirty-one-acre island in Maine overlooking Penobscot Bay evokes the original Shingle Style houses of the area. Its dark-stained shingle exterior wraps around the various forms of its massing; the color connects it to the granite ledges below.

ABOVE LEFT
An arched, jerkinhead gable caps the service wing of the house.

ABOVE RIGHT
Watercolor studies show different color options for window awnings. Renderings by Genevieve Irwin Goelet.

Various details of the façade, however, suggest a more eclectic architectural inheritance, with references to building typologies and elements that might have been experienced on a Grand Tour, including the fluted Doric columns on the kitchen porch, the sgraffito panels above the front door, which are composed of a rough mixture of mortar and stone, gravel, and colored glass, and the elaborate bracketed entrance with a diamante-patterned transom. The ancient doors of Italian churches such as San Costanzo in Perugia and San Francesco in Bologna inspired the paneled front door. The beauty of the island and the architectural allusions of the house coincidentally prompted the new owners to give the house the same name as their predecessors had chosen a century earlier: Isola Bella.

Inside, PPA evoked a similar sense of exoticism and timelessness in collaboration with the designer Alexia Leuschen, who specified the finishes and carried out the interior design. The rooms are brimming with inspirations from the classical world, mediated by the designer's piquant aesthetic sensibilities. PPA organized the main wing of the house, containing the library, living room, and dining room, with strong axes that culminate in the prospect of the water. Throughout the ground floor, the pink Mortadello terrazzo of the floors is inlaid with marble shards from the island. In the rounded stair hall, PPA enhanced the sweeping stair with wood treads that imitate stone in their chiseled profiles. In the dining room, the rustic texture of the terra-cotta pavers laid without grout are counterbalanced by an ornately carved wooden ceiling, recalling that of Hardwick Hall's Long Gallery. Classical touches such as the lattice ceiling and distressed Calacatta Paonazzo marble floor cast the octagonal breakfast room as an aged folly attached to a Shingle Style house.

The design of the service and guest wing is no less evocative. For the kitchen, PPA worked with Leuschen to create the atmosphere of an old-fashioned service quarter and scullery, like that featured in *Gosford Park*. A wall of interior windows overlaid with lattice-patterned stained-oak trim separates the hallway from the main working kitchen, which is clad in white subway tile; the pantry features custom-designed drying racks for the porcelain. At Leuschen's direction, the stark—almost institutional—back stair is housed in a rounded bay with white walls and contrasting stained Douglas fir trim; the arched ceiling

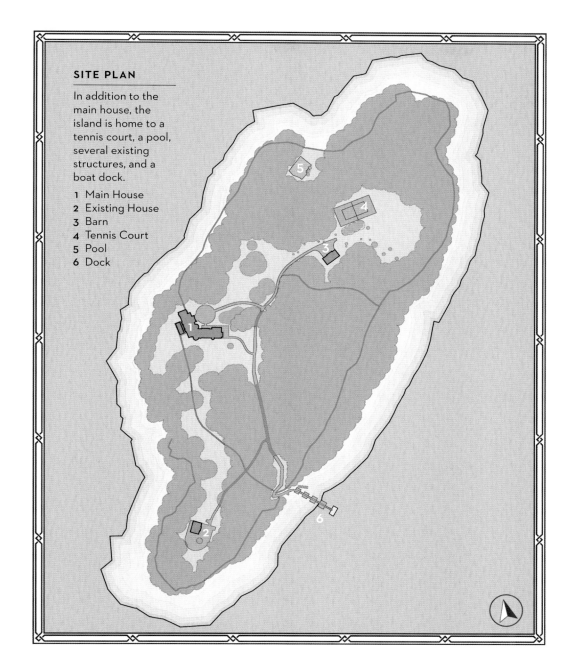

SITE PLAN

In addition to the main house, the island is home to a tennis court, a pool, several existing structures, and a boat dock.

1 Main House
2 Existing House
3 Barn
4 Tennis Court
5 Pool
6 Dock

ABOVE
A narrow shingled porch fronting the kitchen wing is supported by a pair of Doric columns.

ribs dissolve into pilaster caps—a detail often found in Renaissance cloisters. Above, in the long, almost monastic, vaulted guest-bedroom hall with earthy terrazzo floors, PPA carved out apsidal spaces in the dormers. Intentionally devoid of modern conveniences such as air conditioning, built-in lighting, and audio/visual systems, PPA's design suggests that the new house could very well have been built a century earlier.

Accessible only by boat, the island estate includes a handful of preexisting houses—one of which PPA relocated away from the current house site—as well as a tennis court and a rustic saltwater pool overlooking Penobscot Bay. To enhance the landscape, the Madrid-based landscape architect Fernando Caruncho created vistas and walking paths by removing some of the pine and fir trees and adding birch, ash, and Pyrus for seasonal color. Owing to the unforgiving Maine winters and logistics of the island location, much of the house was prefabricated on the mainland to expedite construction.

ABOVE LEFT
The dark shingles and green trim of the exterior connect it to and blend it in with its setting.

ABOVE RIGHT
Like the early Shingle Style houses of McKim, Mead & White, the complication of the massing is offset by the restrained palette of its square-cut and fish-scale cedar shingles.

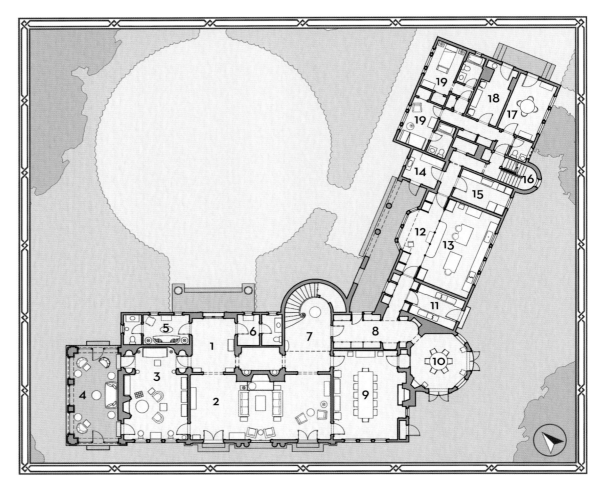

1ST-FLOOR PLAN

The relatively narrow plan of the house allows light and breezes to pass to and from the land and sea sides.

1 Entrance Hall	8 Porcelain Hall	15 Laundry Room
2 Living Room	9 Dining Room	16 Back Stair
3 Library	10 Breakfast Room	17 Staff Mudroom
4 Screened Porch	11 Scullery	18 Luggage Room
5 Women's Cloakroom	12 Kitchen Hall	19 Staff Bedroom
6 Men's Cloakroom	13 Kitchen	
7 Stair Hall	14 Flower Room	

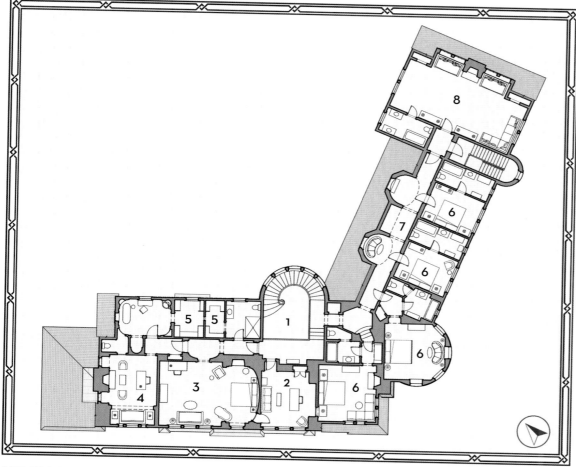

ABOVE AND BELOW
On the entrance side, hand-cut scalloped fish-scale shingles sheathe the round tower, the pepper-pot roof of which is capped by a copper finial. Inspired by the McKim, Mead & White house Southside, in Newport, sgraffito panels made of carved wood framing a rough mixture of mortar with stones, gravel, and glass mixed in for color, announce the front door.

2ND-FLOOR PLAN

The second floor is divided into family and guest quarters.

1 Stair Hall
2 Office
3 Primary Bedroom
4 Boudoir
5 Dressing Room
6 Bedroom
7 Guest Room Hall
8 Nursery

ABOVE LEFT
Throughout the first level
of the house, the pink
Mortadella terrazzo of the
floors is inlaid with shards of
excess marble slabs found
on the island.

ABOVE RIGHT
An enfilade of arches extends
from the stair hall, through
the front hall and library, to
a screened-in porch.

OPPOSITE
A new sweeping wood stair,
set within the curve of a
tower topped by a pepper-
pot roof, has treads chiseled
to imitate diamond-shaped
blocks of stone, giving each
a three-dimensional profile.

LEFT
In the bright living room with acid-lemon-colored bamboo-paneled walls, French doors open onto views of the bay. Classically inspired, operable transoms with curved mullions top the tall French doors.

ABOVE
In the entry hall, the front doors' sculptural diamante panels shaped like pyramids emulate the doors of ancient Italian churches.

ABOVE
With its wood treillage ceiling, distressed antique marble floor, and plaster walls, the breakfast room was designed to feel like a garden gazebo within the house. French doors open onto the lawn and the bay beyond.

OPPOSITE
In the dining room, PPA juxtaposed the rustic texture of the terra-cotta pavers laid without grout with an ornately carved wooden ceiling, recalling that of Hardwick Hall's Long Gallery. It was constructed in four panels on the mainland.

ABOVE LEFT
A bay of windows with diamond panes in the hall that runs parallel to the kitchen overlooks the side porch.

ABOVE RIGHT
The design of the kitchen is intentionally simple, with white subway tile on the walls, stained white oak cabinetry, a green range hood with scalloped white trim, and cement tile floors.

RIGHT
A watercolor study of the stove wall in the kitchen. Rendering by Genevieve Irwin Goelet.

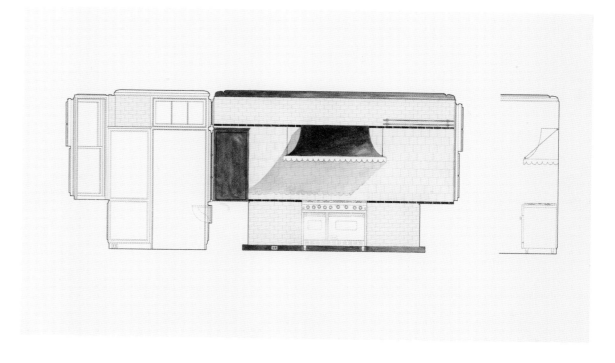

OPPOSITE
A long, vaulted hall leading
to the guest rooms has an
earthy terrazzo floor and
apsidal spaces carved into
the dormers.

ABOVE
Almost monastic in spirit
and inspired by a building
in Venice by Renaissance
architect Mauro Codussi,
the barrel-vaulted back stair,
housed in a rounded bay,
features white walls and
contrasting stained Douglas
fir trim and paneling.

RIGHT
The arched ceiling ribs of
the barrel-vaulted back stair
dissolve into pilaster caps, a
detail found in Renaissance
cloisters.

NEW JERSEY ESTATE

Amid the rolling hills of New Jersey horse country, on the former site of centuries-old family farms, PPA designed a new stone manor. At the turn of the twentieth century, this rural area of the state evolved into a fashionable retreat; much of the farmland was transformed into estates, many of which maintained working farms. With its mix of old farm buildings and large houses—often designed by the well-known architects of the day—buffered by large swaths of open land, this region still feels pristine and untouched. In keeping with the golden age of country houses, the owners of this new house envisioned a classically inspired manor with outbuildings occupying roughly the same footprint as the historic farm structures on the property, which had grown derelict over time.

To maximize the bucolic views of a spring-fed stream and pastures to the east and a river to the west, PPA designed an L-shaped main house with a narrow plan, enabling rooms to have multiple exposures. PPA tempered its impressive size and formality by scaling back the openings and keeping the façades simple, letting the flat surfaces of honey-colored sandstone, with subtly crosshatched grooves, stand as the defining feature. The main block of the house, accentuated by a denticulated cornice, is symmetrical, with a cupola topping the roof above its center door and substantial chimneys flanking the cupola. PPA deployed classical detail sparingly, embellishing only key moments on the façades such as the entry's carved enframement and the porches culminating the plan to the southwest and northeast. Supported by Doric columns, an open-air loggia with a view of a lawn and the woods beyond extends off the less formal wing of the house, where the kitchen, family room, and back stair are located.

Throughout the interior, the ample scale of the rooms allowed PPA to pursue a robust program of moldings and paneling; classical traditions serve as the starting point for a more ebullient and voluptuous style. In the entry hall, wall panels, chair rails, cased arched openings, and Gascogne Blue limestone floors set a formal tone for the axis linking the living room to the southwest and the dining room to the northeast. But the primary axis leads from the front hall through a barrel-vaulted vestibule to the stair hall and out the back door to a flagstone patio. Stretching across two-thirds of the rear of the house, the great oval stair hall is an architectural delight, its detail bathed in light from three generous northwesterly windows. In the Georgian spirit, PPA designed a gracious stair with a carved stringer and balusters and a curling mahogany handrail; it ascends along the curved wall to the upper level. Upstairs, blind

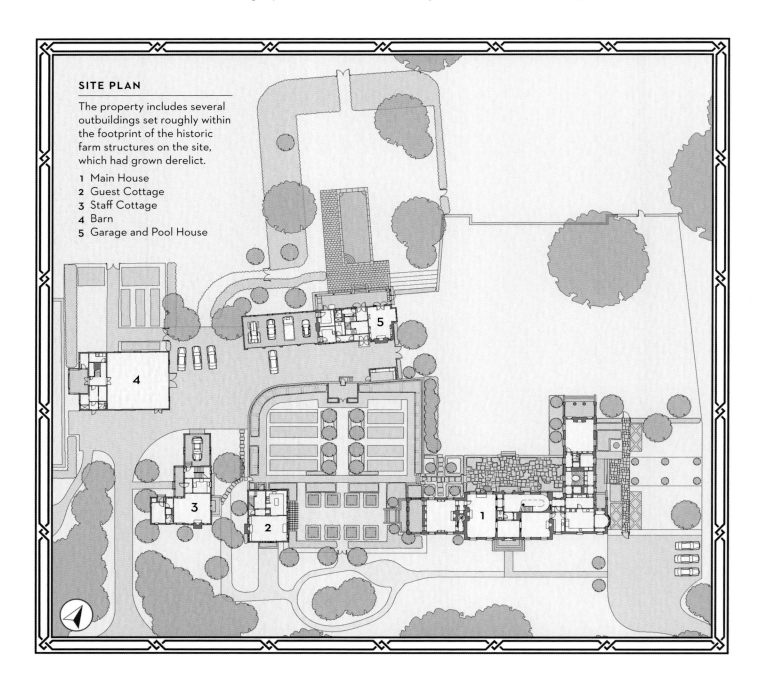

SITE PLAN

The property includes several outbuildings set roughly within the footprint of the historic farm structures on the site, which had grown derelict.

1 Main House
2 Guest Cottage
3 Staff Cottage
4 Barn
5 Garage and Pool House

arches with carved brackets along the southeast wall mirror the location of the windows directly opposite.

In the living and dining rooms, PPA developed a language of details, moldings, and profiles that lends architectural distinction to each space: the living room has subtly curved walls and inventive denticulated moldings; the dining room features an oval-shaped ceiling molding, wainscoting, and acanthus leaf–shaped crown moldings. Though the kitchen wing is less formal, PPA's attention to detail is no less meticulous: the breakfast room has a shallow groin-vaulted ceiling, solid wood paneling, and a bay window; the adjacent kitchen continues in the same vein with wood cabinetry, teak floors, honed Aquario granite countertops, and a custom PPA range hood.

Upstairs, PPA organized the space into wings, allotting the area above the library and living room to the primary suite. With its own entrance off the oval stair hall, it comprises a private hall, sitting room, his-and-her dressing rooms, a large bedroom with windows on either side, a screened sleeping porch overlooking the gardens, and a round stair, secreted away between the bedroom and bathroom, that spirals down to the library below. In the bathroom, a groin vault arches overhead. To the northeast, a pocket door opens off the stair hall to reveal a series of comfortably sized bedrooms for both children and guests, all with ensuite bathrooms. Throughout the interior, the client's choice of furnishings, art, antiques, and color schemes both complement and enhance the architectural design.

PPA clad the exteriors of the outbuildings—a guesthouse, staff cottage, barn, and combined garage and pool house—in a simple, vernacular board and batten. But

TOP
An ink and watercolor wash with gouache touches shows the relationship of the main house to the outbuildings. Rendering by Anton Glikin.

ABOVE
Bay windows draw light into the breakfast room and a bedroom above.

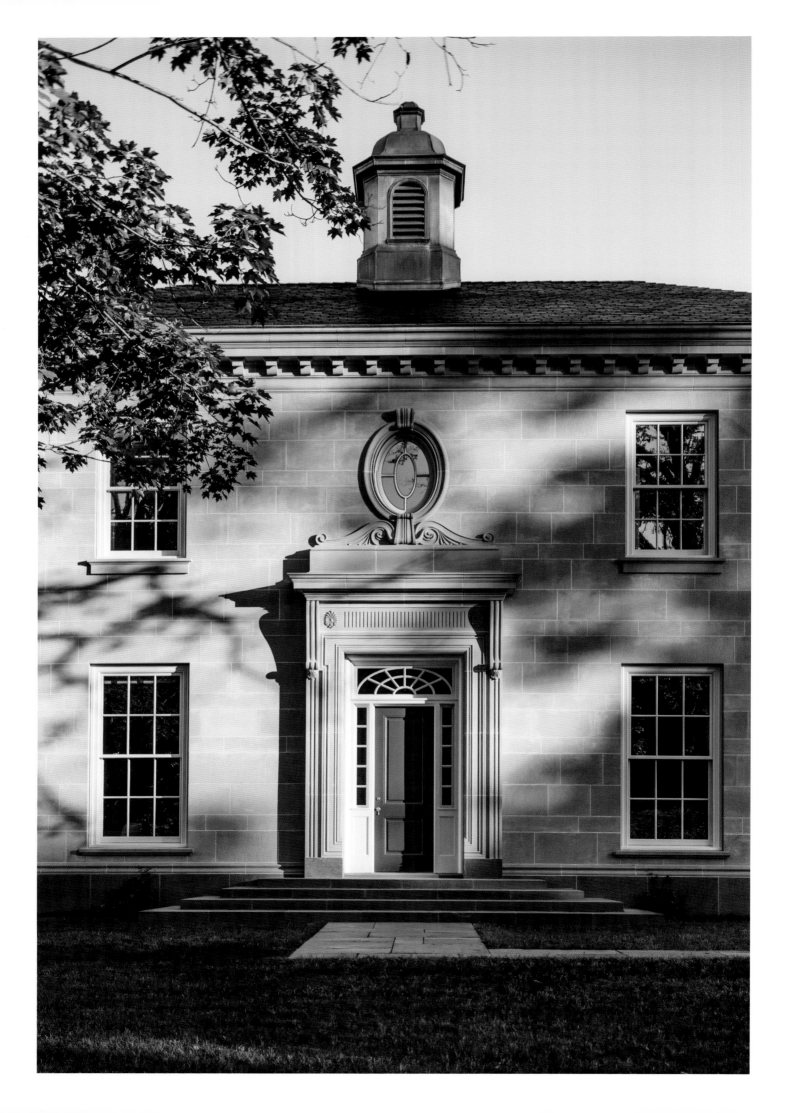

striking a more formal note that references the elevated architecture of the main house is the guest cottage's Colonial Revival doorframe, which PPA designed for an exhibition at the Museum of the City of New York in 2011, *The American Style: Colonial Revival and the Modern Metropolis.* Connecting the cluster of structures with the main house is a large, walled, formal garden designed by landscape architect Miranda Brooks. A grass path through it extends the northeast–southwest axis of the house from the library loggia to the guest cottage. A cross axis extends northwest to a greenhouse, where a cutting garden, rotating beds of vegetables, and wildflowers, surrounded by an undulating brick wall, form a more rustic and romantic enclosure. The views throughout the property and from the house alternate between being highly contained and completely open toward the farm fields and cattle pasture beyond.

OPPOSITE
The sculptural entryway is one of the few places on the otherwise simple exterior where classical themes are fully developed. The large-scale door surround engages the frame of the bull's-eye window above.

OVERLEAF
A porch serving the first-floor library opens onto a lawn flanked by pleached trees; the sleeping porch above enjoys the same green, symmetrical view.

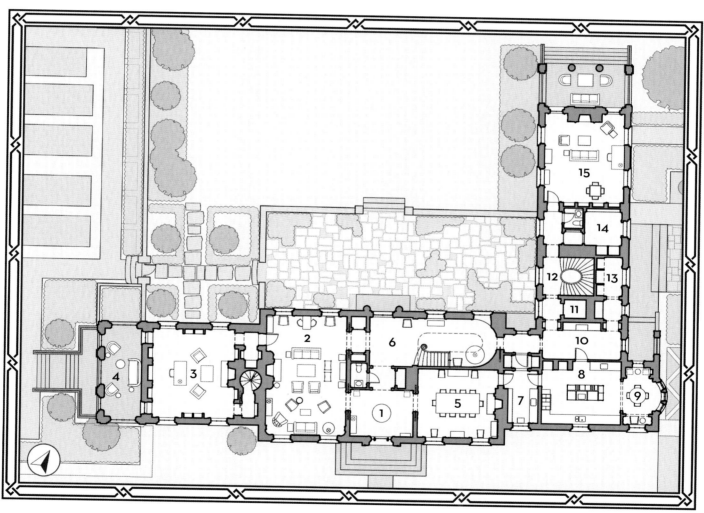

FLOOR PLAN

The thin, L-shaped plan provides multiple exposures in each room.

1 Entrance Hall
2 Living Room
3 Library
4 Screened Porch
5 Dining Room
6 Stair Hall
7 Pantry
8 Kitchen
9 Breakfast Room
10 Mudroom
11 Elevator
12 Back Stair Hall
13 Coat Room
14 Office
15 Family Room

TOP
A less formal board-and-batten vernacular was used for the guest cottage, rebuilt on the foundations of a derelict outbuilding.

LEFT
The vibrant red door and frame of the guest cottage were repurposed from an exhibition on the Colonial Revival that PPA designed for the Museum of the City of New York in 2011.

ABOVE
The rear of the house opens onto a stone terrace, shown here in high summer with plants and herbs bursting from in between the stones. The views on the property range from highly contained (by the garden and architectural walls on the site) to completely open to the farm fields and cattle pastures beyond.

OVERLEAF
Landscape architect Miranda Brooks's enchanting walled garden with string frames for sweet peas knits the main house together with the nearby outbuildings in an elegant way.

ABOVE LEFT AND RIGHT
From the paneled entry hall
with its honed-limestone floor,
an arched opening leads to
a small vaulted hall, paneled
stair hall, and stone terrace
beyond (left), and pocket
doors open into the living
room (right).

OPPOSITE
An enfilade of tall arched
openings connects the main
rooms in the house. In the
dining room, the generous
archway is centered on
the mantel.

OVERLEAF LEFT
The ample scale of the rooms
allows for a robust program
of moldings and paneling. In
the living room, the corners
of the chimney breast are
sculpted in curved segments,
forming a projection of the
ceiling cornice.

OVERLEAF RIGHT
In the dining room, moldings
sculpted to evoke acanthus
leaves engage the underside
of the cornice.

OPPOSITE
A plaster cross vault marks the center of the oak-trimmed breakfast bay.

ABOVE
The vaulted kitchen is finished with oak cabinetry, teak floors, a glazed stainless-steel range hood, and Aquario granite countertops.

ABOVE
The rear stair spirals down to a mudroom with a rustic, checkerboard-patterned stone tile floor.

RIGHT
The family room off the kitchen is lit by large, six-over-six double-hung windows. Tall doors on either side of the chimney breast connect the space to a porch overlooking the lush landscape.

OPPOSITE
The curve of the main stair echoes the curved shape of the stair hall.

ABOVE
In the upstairs hallway, paneling frames an elliptical window that pivots on its center axis on hinges that PPA designed in collaboration with Lowe Hardware in Maine.

RIGHT
In the curved upstairs stair hall, blind arches reflect the arches set within the window bays facing the garden.

LEFT
In a small bedroom above the main entrance, paneling frames an ample elliptical bull's-eye window.

ABOVE
In a groin-vaulted bathroom, the vanity and Aquario granite bathtub fit neatly into arched niches.

SUMMER HOUSE ON EASTERN LONG ISLAND

Once the home of the Namaganesett Club, an early 1900s lawn tennis club for a beach community, the design of this 7,000-square-foot house and its outbuildings reflects the architectural informality of the surrounding historic seaside hamlet: a mix of early American farmhouses and simple, turn-of-the-twentieth-century shingled cottages. With its wide porches and low-lying, enveloping roof, the house had an idiosyncratic and unassuming charm that appealed to the owners, evoking fond memories of childhood summers by the ocean. Although initially just a summer rental, the owners quickly acquired the property and asked PPA to transform the quirky house into a luxurious beach cottage as the center of a family compound.

The house had recently been renovated by a local builder who had reduced rooms that would have originally been paneled in simple pine board to sheetrock boxes. In the spirit of a rambling summer house with various accretions made over time, the interior was deceptively large, with a series of charming dormered bedrooms and bathrooms tucked into the eaves. Streamlining the plan, PPA transformed a gloomy screened porch off the kitchen into a sunny summer dining room and added a new bay window in the playroom. By reducing and reconfiguring the overscale central stair, PPA was able to recapture space and create separation between the primary suite, guest suite, and secondary bedrooms and rejigger the plan so each would have an ensuite bathroom. PPA introduced newly designed moldings and paneling but retained many of the rooms' original features, including the prominent wood ceiling beams on the first floor. For the décor, the clients brought on Jacques Grange to design bright, unfussy rooms with a mix of high and low furnishings. His soothing color scheme complements

PRECEDING PAGES
A pair of shingled pool pavilions, housing a kitchenette and changing room, are joined by chinoiserie fretwork.

RIGHT
The house occupies a structure built in the early twentieth century as a lawn tennis club for a beach community in eastern Long Island. Its wide porches and low-lying, enveloping roof are typical of the low-key shingled cottages of the early 1900s.

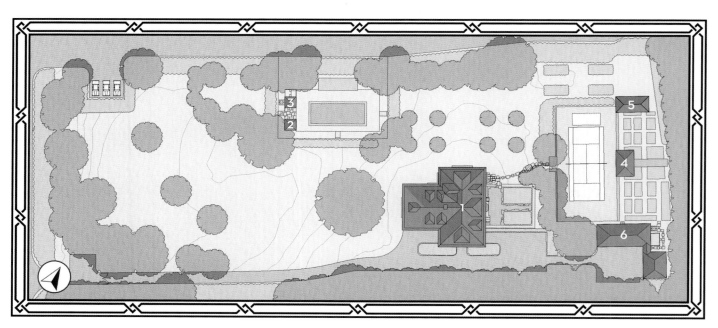

SITE PLAN

Set back from the road, the house overlooks a deep. undulating lawn.

1 Main House
2 Kitchenette

3 Changing Room
4 Tennis Pavilion

5 Exercise Studio
   and Tennis Storage
6 Guest Cottage

the simple lines of PPA's design; the green of the floors, beams, and trim—inspired by a lichen-covered piece of bark he had found on the property—ties the interiors and architecture to the gardens and landscape beyond.

Set back from the road by a deep, undulating lawn, the grounds were spacious enough to accommodate a number of ancillary buildings as well as lush flower and organic vegetable gardens designed by Miranda Brooks. For both the new and the renovated structures on the property, PPA took cues from the main house's low-slung hipped roof and tucked-in dormers and employed the same simple, crisp lines of the shingled vernacular. At the front of the property, PPA worked with Edmund Hollander to incorporate a new pool and a trellis flanked by a pair of shingled pavilions; one is a changing room and the other houses a retro kitchenette and ice cream counter. At the rear, PPA designed an open tennis pavilion and renovated an existing guest cottage and garage, which now enclose Brooks's vibrant kitchen garden. Another shed was transformed into an exercise studio with wood-lined walls and exposed ceiling beams. Accessed by an oystershell-paved drive that runs deep into the lot, this charming summer retreat is screened from the road by Hollander's verdant hedges and trees.

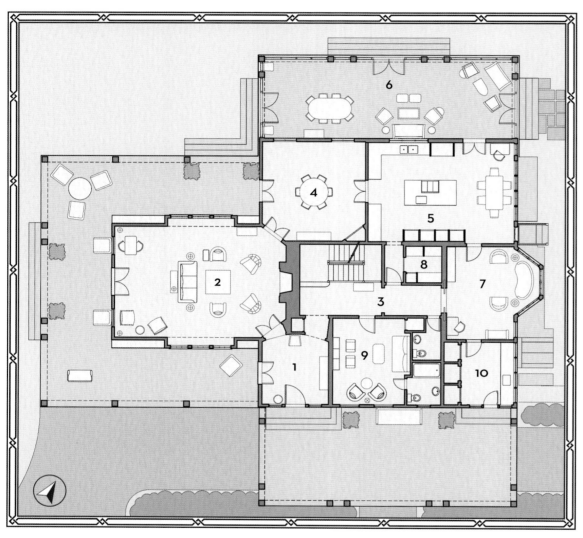

FLOOR PLAN

PPA streamlined the plan to facilitate an easy flow between rooms; screened and open-air porches open off of all of the rooms on the first floor of the house.

1 Entrance Hall
2 Living Room
3 Stair Hall

4 Dining Room
5 Kitchen
6 Screened Porch

7 Playroom
8 Pantry

9 Den
10 Mud Room

An existing porch was screened in to transform it into a mosquito-proof outdoor seating and dining space.

ABOVE LEFT
The front door opens into a bright hall enhanced by new moldings and interior designer Jacques Grange's green-painted mullions.

ABOVE RIGHT
PPA reduced and reconfigured the existing overscale central stair and added attic-story windows.

OPPOSITE
PPA's simple applied moldings on the dining room ceiling form a pattern inspired by a house on the Bosporus.

COUNTRY

ABOVE
PPA retained many of the house's original features, including the prominent wood ceiling beams on the first floor, painted a summery green inspired by a piece of lichen-covered bark that Grange had found on the property.

RIGHT
French doors in the living room lead to an open-air porch that wraps around all three sides of the room.

ABOVE
One of the pool pavilions houses a kitchenette that doubles as an ice cream parlor.

OPPOSITE
The beadboard walls, painted floors, and French doors in a sunlit corner of the kitchen are redolent of summer.

OPPOSITE
In the new plan, PPA recaptured space to create a private primary
suite, tucked beneath the low-slung roof.

ABOVE
A simple bathroom with wood floors and a freestanding tub is
nestled in an attic gable.

PROJECTS

SUMMER HOUSE ON EASTERN LONG ISLAND (*see pages 278–91*)

Suffolk County, New York / 2009
Partner-in-Charge: Peter Pennoyer
Design: Mark Herring
Project Manager: Pui Ng
Associates: Todd Brickell, Craig Doyle,
    Oscar Carrera, Sean Blackwell, Aaron Rigby,
    Benjamin Sirota
Interior Design: Jacques Grange Interiors
Landscape: Hollander Design Landscape Architects
    and Miranda Books Landscape Design

TOWNHOUSE ON EAST 75TH STREET

New York, New York / 2009
Partner-in-Charge: Peter Pennoyer
Design: Anton Glikin and Mark Herring
Project Manager: Jennifer Gerakaris
Associates: Cecilia Rodgers, Lucas Hafeli,
    Cory Roffelsen
Interior Design: Jacques Grange Interiors

ART DECO ON THE RIVER
(*see pages 62–69*)

New York, New York / 2010
Partner-in-Charge: Peter Pennoyer
Design: Peter Pennoyer
Project Manager: Pui Ng
Associates: Cory Roffelsen, Lucas Hafeli, F. Patrick
    Mohan, John Gibbons, Cecilia Rodgers
Interior Design: Victoria Hagan Interiors

TOWNHOUSE ON EAST 80TH STREET

New York, New York / 2011
Partner-in-Charge: Elizabeth Graziolo
Design: Gregory Gilmartin
Project Manager: Timothy Kelly
Associate: Cleary Shea

TOWNHOUSE ON EAST
80TH STREET

STORE FOR DAVID WEBB JEWELERS AT 942 MADISON AVENUE

New York, New York / 2011
Partner-in-Charge: Peter Pennoyer
Design: Peter Pennoyer
Associate: Cecilia Rodgers
Interior Design: Katie Ridder Inc.

EXHIBITION: *THE AMERICAN STYLE: COLONIAL REVIVAL AND THE MODERN METROPOLIS*

Museum of the City of New York, New York / 2011
Exhibition Design: Peter Pennoyer Architects
Design: Mark Herring
Associates: Cecilia Rodgers and R. Nathaniel Brooks
Curators: Donald Albrecht and Thomas Mellins

HOUSE ON GEORGICA POND
(*see pages 226–37*)

Suffolk County, New York / 2012
Partner-in-Charge: Jennifer Gerakaris
Design: Mark Herring and Nebojsa Savic
Project Manager: Daniel Berkman
Associates: Lucas Hafeli and Cecilia Rodgers
Landscape: Edwina von Gal
Interior Design: Matthew Patrick Smyth
    Interior Design

FIFTH AVENUE MAISONETTE
(see pages 34–47)

New York, New York / 2012
Partner-in-Charge: Peter Pennoyer
Design: Mark Herring
Project Manager: Todd Brickell
Associates: R. Nathaniel Brooks, Oscar Carrera,
 Christian Foster, Cory Roffelsen,
 Daniel Berkman
Interior Design: Peter Pennoyer Architects
Interior Design Director: Anne Foxley
Interior Design Associates: Alejandra Kelly,
 Tharon Anderson, Catherine Collins

STONE COTTAGE

Greenwich, Connecticut / 2012
Partner-in-Charge: Peter Pennoyer
Design: Peter Pennoyer
Project Manager: Joseph Pagac
Interior Design: Katie Ridder Inc.
Landscape: Hollander Design Landscape Architects

A HOUSE IN THE COUNTRY

Millbrook, New York / 2013
Partners-in-Charge: Peter Pennoyer and James Taylor
Design: Gregory Gilmartin
Project Manager: James Taylor
Associates: Matthew Cummings, Arthur Rollin, Cecilia
 Rodgers, Timothy Kelly, Genevieve Irwin Goelet
Interior Design: Katie Ridder Inc.
Landscape: Hollander Design Landscape Architects
Garden: Katie Ridder

MUSEUM MILE DUPLEX
(see pages 80–89)

New York, New York / 2013
Partner-in-Charge: Peter Pennoyer
Design: Mark Herring
Project Manager: Todd Brickell
Associates: R. Nathaniel Brooks, Cecilia Rodgers,
 Christian Foster
Interior Design: S.R. Gambrel, Inc.

ISOLA BELLA *(see pages 238–53)*

Penobscot Bay, Maine / 2013
Partner-in-Charge: Peter Pennoyer
Design: Gregory Gilmartin and James Taylor
Project Manager: James Taylor
Associates: John Gibbons, Matthew Cummings,
 Nebojsa Savic, Lucas Hafeli, F. Patrick Mohan,
 Cecilia Rodgers, Cleary Shea, Jennifer Gerakaris
Interior Design: Alexia Leuschen
Landscape: Caruncho Garden & Architecture

PROPOSAL FOR A LENDING LIBRARY ADDITION TO THE NEW YORK PUBLIC LIBRARY *(see pages 16–17)*

New York, New York / 2014
Partner-in-Charge: Peter Pennoyer
Associate: Sam Roche

BRONZE BASES FOR ANTIQUE PIETRA DURA PANELS

2014
Design: Anton Glikin

GREENWICH VILLAGE TOWNHOUSE
(see pages 110–23)

New York, New York / 2014
Partner-in-Charge: Thomas P. R. Nugent
Design: Gregory Gilmartin
Project Manager: Joseph Pagac
Associates: Thomas Lamontagne, Cleary Shea,
 Cecilia Rodgers, Mark Herring
Interior Design: Shawn Henderson
Landscape: Madison Cox Associates with
 The Organic Gardener

MADISON AVENUE APARTMENT

New York, New York / 2014
Partner-in-Charge: Peter Pennoyer
Design: R. Nathaniel Brooks
Project Manager: R. Nathaniel Brooks
Associates: Cory Roffelsen, Meeghan Hart,
 Rachel Edrington, Amelia Enslee, John Gibbons
Interior Design: Peter Pennoyer Architects
Interior Design Directors: R. Nathaniel Brooks and
 Anne Foxley
Interior Design Associates: Tharon Anderson,
 Dorynne Brock, Catherine Collins

BRONZE BASES FOR ANTIQUE
PIETRA DURA PANELS

MADISON AVENUE APARTMENT

FIFTH AVENUE APARTMENT

FIFTH AVENUE APARTMENT

New York, New York / 2014
Partner-in-Charge: Elizabeth Graziolo
Design: Gregory Gilmartin and Peter Pennoyer
Project Manager: R. Nathaniel Brooks
Associate: Cory Roffelsen
Interior Design: Katie Ridder Inc.

EXHIBITION: *DAVID WEBB: SOCIETY'S JEWELER*

Norton Museum of Art, West Palm Beach,
    Florida / 2014
Partner-in-Charge: Peter Pennoyer
Design: Mark Herring

GARDEN VILLAGE AT WOLONG BAY

Dalian, China / 2014
Partner-in-Charge: Elizabeth Graziolo
Design: Anton Glikin
Project Manager: Ying Liu
Associates: Paloma Pajares, Cory Roffelsen,
    Timothy Kelly

BEAUX-ARTS ESTATE

Dalian, China / 2014
Partner-in-Charge: Elizabeth Graziolo
Design: Anton Glikin
Project Manager: Ying Liu
Associate: Timothy Kelly

EXHIBITION: *DAVID WEBB: SOCIETY'S JEWELER*

GARDEN VILLAGE AT WOLONG BAY

BEAUX-ARTS ESTATE

PARK AVENUE APARTMENT

New York, New York / 2014
Partner-in-Charge: Elizabeth Graziolo
Design: Mark Herring and R. Nathaniel Brooks
Project Manager: R. Nathaniel Brooks
Interior Design: Peter Pennoyer Architects
Interior Design Director: R. Nathaniel Brooks
Interior Design Associates: Alice Engel, Lily Wick,
    Kate McElhiney, Cara Wasserman, Callie Nelson,
    Madeline Nastala, India Dial, Nicole Violé

FIFTH AVENUE DUPLEX

New York, New York / 2014
Partner-in-Charge: Elizabeth Graziolo
Design: Peter Pennoyer and Elizabeth Graziolo
Project Manager: Elizabeth Graziolo
Associates: Catherine Kirchhoff and Cory Roffelsen
Interior Design: Louise W. Cronan Interior
    Decoration

744 MADISON AVENUE (151 EAST 78TH STREET SALES OFFICE)

New York, New York / 2014
Partner-in-Charge: Elizabeth Graziolo
Project Manager: James Teese Jr.
Associates: Catherine Kirchhoff, Rachel Edrington
Interior Design: Peter Pennoyer Architects
Interior Design Directors: R. Nathaniel Brooks and
    Peter Pennoyer
Interior Design Associates: Nicole Violé,
    Dorynne Brock

NEW JERSEY ESTATE *(see pages 254–77)*

New Jersey /2015
Partner-in-Charge: Peter Pennoyer
Design: Anton Glikin and Gregory Gilmartin
Project Manager: Nebojsa Savic
Associates: Matthew Cairo, Francine Hsu Davis,
    Amelia Enslee, Xuan Luo, F. Patrick Mohan
Landscape: Miranda Brooks Landscape Design

LADIES' MILE TRIPLEX *(see pages 70–79)*

New York, New York / 2015
Partner-in-Charge: Thomas P. R. Nugent
Design: Gregory Gilmartin and Peter Pennoyer
Project Manager: Cleary Shea
Associates: Nicholas Schroeder and John Gibbons
Interior Design: Katie Ridder Inc.

FIFTH AVENUE DUPLEX

New York, New York / 2015
Partner-in-Charge: Peter Pennoyer
Design: Mark Herring
Project Manager: Todd Brickell
Associates: Meeghan Hart and John Gibbons
Interior Design: Jennifer Garrigues Inc.

HOUSE ON THE NORTH SHORE

St. James, New York / 2015
Partner-in-Charge: Thomas P. R. Nugent
Design: Gregory Gilmartin
Project Manager: Francine Hsu Davis
Associate: Thomas Lamontagne

OCEANFRONT MANSION

Palm Beach, Florida / 2015
Partner-in-Charge: Thomas P. R. Nugent
Design: Timothy Kelly
Project Manager: Timothy Kelly
Associates: John Gibbons and Nicholas Schroeder
Interior Design: Katie Ridder Inc.
Landscape: Andrés Paradelo

MANSIONS ON THE PEAK

Hong Kong / 2015
Partners-in-Charge: Elizabeth Graziolo and
    Peter Pennoyer
Design: Mark Herring
Project Manager: Ying Liu
Associates: Philip Davis, Scott Varian, Sebastian von
    Marschall, James Teese Jr.
Landscape: Hollander Design Landscape Architects

OFFICES OF PETER PENNOYER ARCHITECTS AT 136 MADISON AVENUE *(see pages 12–13)*

New York, New York / 2015
Partner-in-Charge: James Taylor
Design: Gregory Gilmartin and Peter Pennoyer
Project Manager: Cleary Shea
Associates: Christian Foster, Daniel Berkman,
    John Gibbons, Rachel Edrington, Ram Krishnan,
    Xuan Luo, Sebastian von Marschall, Lisa Schumaker
Interior Design Director: Peter Pennoyer
Interior Design Associates: R. Nathaniel Brooks,
    Dorynne Brock, Michelle Ficker, Alice Engel

FIFTH AVENUE APARTMENT

New York, New York / 2016
Partner-in-Charge: Elizabeth Graziolo
Design: Mark Herring
Project Manager: Catherine Kirchhoff
Associates: John Gibbons, Kathryn Fowler,
    Ying Liu
Interior Design: Tom Scheerer Inc.

STONE HOUSE

Westchester County, New York / 2016
Partner-in-Charge: Elizabeth Graziolo
Design: Peter Pennoyer
Project Manager: Joseph Pagac
Associates: Rowan Sloss and John Gibbons
Interior Design: Katie Ridder Inc.
Landscape: Doyle Herman Design Associates

LONG ISLAND BEACH HOUSE
(see pages 188–201)

Suffolk County, New York / 2016
Partner-in-Charge: James Taylor
Design: James Taylor
Project Manager: Christopher Pizzichemi
Associates: Christian Foster, John Gibbons,
    Philip Davis, Rachel Edrington, Daniel Heath,
    Matthew Cummings
Interior Design: Victoria Hagan Interiors
Landscape: Hollander Design Landscape Architects

SEVENTEENTH-CENTURY GUESTHOUSE
(see pages 202–11)

Suffolk County, New York / 2016
Partner-in-Charge: James Taylor
Design: James Taylor
Project Manager: Christopher Pizzichemi
Associates: Christian Foster, John Gibbons,
    Philip Davis, Rachel Edrington, Daniel Heath,
    Matthew Cummings, Arthur Rollin
Interior Design: Robert Stilin
Landscape: Hollander Design Landscape Architects

151 EAST 78TH STREET
(see pages 130–35)

New York, New York / 2016
Partners-in-Charge: Elizabeth Graziolo and
    Peter Pennoyer
Design: Gregory Gilmartin, Elizabeth Graziolo,
    James Taylor
Project Manager: James Teese Jr.
Associates: Joseph Pagac, Ying Liu,
    Catherine Kirchhoff, Rachel Edrington,
    Christopher Pizzichemi, John Gibbons,
    Philip Davis
Interior Design: Peter Pennoyer Architects
Interior Design Director: R. Nathaniel Brooks
Interior Design Associates: Nicole Violé,
    Dorynne Brock, Michelle Ficker, Genevieve Irwin
    Goelet, Lisa Cady, Rena Sarant

OFFICES OF PETER PENNOYER ARCHITECTS
AT 136 MADISON AVENUE

STONE HOUSE

CLARKSON STREET

EXHIBITION: *FOLLIES, FUNCTION & FORM: IMAGINING OLANA'S SUMMER HOUSE*

HARDWARE DESIGN

CLARKSON STREET (UNBUILT)

New York, New York /2016
Partner-in-Charge: Elizabeth Graziolo
Design: Benjamin Salling
Project Managers: Joseph Pagac and Madison Head
Associates: John Gibbons, Meeghan Hart,
    Philip Davis, Todd Brickell, Omar Walker,
    Sebastian von Marschall

EXHIBITION: *FOLLIES, FUNCTION & FORM: IMAGINING OLANA'S SUMMER HOUSE*

Olana State Historic Site, Hudson, New York / 2016
Design: Anton Glikin

BRICK HOUSE

Southampton, New York / 2016
Partner-in-Charge: James Taylor
Design: Gregory Gilmartin, R. Nathaniel Brooks,
    Timothy Kelly
Project Manager: Elisa Cuaron
Associates: Marshall Knutson, Rachel Edrington,
    Adam Castiglione, Rowan Sloss, John Gibbons,
    Daniel Trumble, Philip Davis, Ram Krishnan,
    Xuan Luo
Interior Design: Peter Pennoyer Architects
Interior Design Directors: R. Nathaniel Brooks and
    Alice Engel
Interior Design Associates: India Dial,
    Michelle Ficker, Kate McElhiney, Madeline
    Nastala, Callie Nelson, Lily Wick
Landscape: Michael Derrig, Landscape Details

HARDWARE DESIGN *(see page 19)*

2017–2020
Design: James Taylor and Peter Pennoyer

PARK AVENUE APARTMENT

New York, New York / 2017
Partner-in-Charge: Peter Pennoyer
Design: R. Nathaniel Brooks
Project Manager: Cory Roffelsen
Associates: Daniel Trumble, John Gibbons,
    Nicholas Schroeder, Philip Davis
Interior Design: KR Design Group

NEW VILLA ON A HISTORIC LONG ISLAND ESTATE *(see pages 212–25)*

Suffolk County, New York / 2017
Partner-in-Charge: James Taylor
Design: Gregory Gilmartin
Project Managers: Nebojsa Savic and
    Matthew Cairo
Associates: John Gibbons, Jordan Kasperson,
    Xuan Luo
Interior Design: Katie Ridder Inc.
Landscape: LaGuardia Design Group

CANDELA DUPLEX *(see pages 22–33)*

New York, New York / 2017
Partner-in-Charge: Peter Pennoyer
Design: Mark Herring
Project Manager: Pui Ng
Associates: Nicholas Schroeder, Ying Liu,
    Todd Brickell, Thomas Lamontagne, Nebojsa Savic,
    Meeghan Hart, John Gibbons, James Taylor,
    Daniel Trumble
Interior Design: Peter Pennoyer Architects
Interior Design Director: R. Nathaniel Brooks
Interior Design Associates: Alice Engel, Rena Sarant,
    Elizabeth Theriot, Bonnie Hoeker

HOUSE ON GEORGICA POND

East Hampton, New York / 2017
Partner-in-Charge: Jennifer Gerakaris
Design: Benjamin Salling
Project Manager: Daniel Berkman
Associates: Cory Roffelsen, Daniel Trumble,
    Matthew Enquist, Kathryn Fowler, John Gibbons,
    Nicholas Schroeder, Philip Davis, Jordan Kasperson
Interior Design: GWdesign
Landscape: Hollander Design Landscape Architects

ROWDY MEADOW *(see page 19)*

Hunting Valley, Ohio / 2018
Partner-in-Charge: James Taylor
Design: Gregory Gilmartin
Project Manager: Lucas Hafeli
Associates: Steven Aldridge, Matthew Cummings,
    Philip Davis, Rachel Edrington, John Gibbons,
    Anton Glikin, Daniel Heath, Timothy Kelly, Ying Liu
Interior Design: Peter Pennoyer Architects
Interior Design Directors: R. Nathaniel Brooks and
    Alice Engel
Interior Design Associates: Michelle Ficker,
    Bonnie Hoeker, Rena Sarant, Elizabeth Theriot,
    Lily Wick
Landscape: Reed Hilderbrand LLC

NOB HILL APARTMENT TOWER (UNBUILT)

San Francisco, California / 2018
Partner-in-Charge: Peter Pennoyer
Design: Benjamin Salling

EXHIBITION: *ELEGANCE IN THE SKY: THE ARCHITECTURE OF ROSARIO CANDELA*

Museum of the City of New York, New York / 2018
Partner-in-Charge: Peter Pennoyer
Design: Mark Herring
Associates: Nirui Kang, Steven Worthington,
  Benjamin Salling, Armon White, Benjamin Salling,
  Colin Slaten, Steven Worthington
Architectural Historian: Anne Walker
Curator: Donald Albrecht

RAILINGS AND GATE FOR THE NAVE OF ST. THOMAS CHURCH ON FIFTH AVENUE (UNBUILT)

New York, New York / 2018
Partner-in-Charge: James Taylor
Associate: Steven Aldridge

APARTMENT ON CENTRAL PARK WEST

New York, New York / 2018
Interior Design: Peter Pennoyer Architects
Interior Design Director: Alice Engel
Interior Design Associate: Lily Wick

STONE ESTATE

Michigan / 2019
Partner-in-Charge: Elizabeth Graziolo
Design: Timothy Kelly
Project Manager: Rami Idlby
Associates: Miraya Fabregas, John Gibbons,
  Marshall Knutson, Colin Slaten, Maria Cohn

KIPS BAY DESIGNER SHOWHOUSE 2019
(see page 18)

New York, New York / 2019
Interior Design: Peter Pennoyer Architects
Interior Design Director: Alice Engel
Interior Design Associates: Cara Wasserstrom and
  Lily Wick

NORTH SHORE ESTATE *(see pages 160–87)*

Massachusetts / 2019
Partner-in-Charge: Jennifer Gerakaris
Design: Benjamin Salling
Project Manager: Kathryn Fowler
Associates: Cory Roffelsen, John Gibbons,
  Matthew Cairo, Nicholas Schroeder, Philip Davis,
  Ram Krishnam, Colin Slaten
Interior Design: Max Rollitt
Landscape: Laura Gibson Landscape Design

TWO TOWNHOUSES INTO ONE
(see pages 92–109)

New York, New York / 2019
Partner-in-Charge: Jennifer Gerakaris
Design: Gregory Gilmartin
Project Manager: Thomas Lamontagne
Associates: Lucas Hafeli and Madison Head
Interior Design: Giovanna Bianco

PARK AVENUE DUPLEX

New York, New York / 2019
Partner-in-Charge: Elizabeth Graziolo
Design: Mark Herring, Gregory Gilmartin,
  Elizabeth Graziolo
Project Manager: Cleary Shea
Associates: Nicholas Schroeder, Lisa Schumaker,
  Sebastian von Marschall, Coltan Severson,
  John Gibbons, Meeghan Hart, Philip Davis,
  Omar Walker
Interior Design: Julie Hillman Design

ARTS AND CRAFTS HOUSE IN OHIO
(see pages 138–59)

Chagrin Valley, Ohio / 2019
Partner-in-Charge: Thomas P. R. Nugent
Design: Timothy Kelly
Project Manager: Timothy Kelly
Associates: Adam Castiglione, John Gibbons,
  Meeghan Hart, Anton Glikin
Interior Design: Redd Kaihoi LLC
Landscape: Hollander Design Landscape Architects

SHINGLE-STYLE HOUSE

East Hampton, New York / 2019
Partner-in-Charge: James Taylor
Design: James Taylor and Peter Pennoyer
Project Managers: Elisa Cuaron, Rachel Edrington,
  John Gibbons
Associate: Marshall Knutson
Interior Design: Susan Salzman
Landscape: LaGuardia Design Landscape Architecture

GREENWICH VILLAGE TOWNHOUSE

New York, New York / 2019
Partner-in-Charge: Elizabeth Graziolo
Design: Anton Glikin
Project Manager: James Teese Jr.
Associates: Karile Nefaite, Christopher Pizzichemi,
  John Gibbons, Philip Davis, Rowan Sloss,
  Madison Head, Hayley Fazio
Interior Design: Dan Fink Studio

FIFTH AVENUE APARTMENT

New York, New York / 2019
Partner-in-Charge: James Taylor
Design: Mark Herring
Project Managers: Nicholas Schroeder and Pui Ng
Associate: John Gibbons
Interior Design: Peter Pennoyer Architects
Interior Design: Alice Engel
Interior Design Associates: Elizabeth Theriot and
  Cara Wasserstrom

EXHIBITION: *ELEGANCE IN THE SKY: THE ARCHITECTURE OF ROSARIO CANDELA*

CLASSICAL HOUSE

APARTMENT ON CENTRAL PARK SOUTH

New York, New York / 2019
Interior Design: Peter Pennoyer Architects
Interior Design Director: Alice Engel
Interior Design Associates: Michelle Ficker, Bonnie
    Hoeker, Tori Thorgersen, Dorynne Brock

CLASSICAL HOUSE

Rhode Island / 2020
Partner-in-Charge: Thomas P. R. Nugent
Design: Gregory Gilmartin
Project Managers: Nebosja Savic and
    Thomas Lamontagne
Associates: John Gibbons, Nicholas Schroeder, Philip
    Davis, Marshall Knutson, Sebastian von Marschall,
    Benjamin Salling
Interior Design: Franklin & Company Design
    Associates
Landscape: Madison Cox Associates and Garden 26

FIFTH AVENUE APARTMENT

New York, New York / 2020
Partner-in-Charge: Elizabeth Graziolo
Design: Mark Herring
Project Manager: Daniel Trumble
Associates: Cleary Shea, John Gibbons, Matthew
    Cairo, Philip Davis, Steven Aldridge, Ying Liu,
    Emmitt Moore, Nirui Kang, Steven Worthington
Interior Design: Jacques Grange Interiors

HOUSE IN BEL AIR

HOUSE IN BEL AIR

Los Angeles, California / 2020
Partners-in-Charge: Peter Pennoyer and
    Jennifer Gerakaris
Design: Eero Schultz
Project Manager: James Teese Jr.
Associates: John Gibbons, Crystal Hanley, Philip
    Davis, Karile Nefaite, Kate McElhiney

KENTUCKY HORSE FARM

KENTUCKY HORSE FARM

Lexington, Kentucky / 2020
Partner-in-Charge: Thomas P. R. Nugent
Design: Timothy Kelly
Project Manager: Cleary Shea
Associates: John Gibbons, Philip Davis, Rowan Sloss,
    Henry Hofmann, Colin Slaten, Maria Cohn

MOYNIHAN TRAIN HALL CLOCK

(see pages 14–15)
New York, New York / 2020
Partner-in-Charge: Peter Pennoyer
Design: Steven Worthington
Project Manager: Colin Richardson
Associates: Colin Slaten, William Barker, John
    Gibbons, Philip Davis, Anika Tsapatsaris

CLASSICAL STONE HOUSE

HOUSE ON THE BAY (UNBUILT)

Virginia Beach, Virginia / 2020
Partner-in-Charge: Peter Pennoyer
Design: Timothy Kelly
Associates: Karile Nefaite, Colin Slaten, John Gibbons

THE BENSON *(see pages 124–29)*

New York, New York / 2021
Partner-in-Charge: Elizabeth Graziolo
Design: Gregory Gilmartin, Benjamin Salling,
    Peter Pennoyer
Project Manager: Colin Richardson
Associates: Rami Idlby, John Gibbons, James Teese Jr.,
    Matthew Cairo, Myrat Saryyev, Madison Head,
    Emmitt Moore, Janice Rivera-Hall, Liam Hullihan,
    Armon White, Steven Worthington, Henry Hofmann,
    Colin Slaten, Zenja Draca, Peter Mielnicki,
    Moataz Bashir

PARK AVENUE APARTMENT

New York, New York / 2021
Partner-in-Charge: Peter Pennoyer
Design: Peter Pennoyer
Project Manager: Karile Nefaite
Associates: Nicholas Schroeder, Colin Slaten,
    Daniel Trumble, John Gibbons, Philip Davis
Interior Design: Peter Pennoyer Architects
Interior Design Director: Alice Engel
Interior Design Associates: Kate McElhiney,
    Madeline Nastala, Callie Nelson, Cara Wasserstom

CLASSICAL STONE HOUSE (UNBUILT)

Alpine, New Jersey / 2021
Partner-in-Charge: Thomas P. R. Nugent
Design: Gregory Gilmartin
Project Manager: Timothy Kelly
Associates: Colin Slaten, James Teese Jr., John
    Gibbons, Philip Davis, Hayley Fazio, Maria Cohn,
    Kate McElhiney, Zhian Yin, Elizabeth Reeves,
    Megan Stout, Jerry Yan
Landscape: Madison Cox Associates and Garden 26

COUNTRY HOUSE

Connecticut / 2021
Partner-in-Charge: Jennifer Gerakaris
Design: Benjamin Salling
Project Manager: Kathryn Fowler
Associates: John Gibbons, Philip Davis,
    Thomas Lamontagne, Jacob Lee
Interior Design: Demisch Danant

APARTMENT ON EAST 72ND STREET

New York, New York / 2021
Interior Design: Peter Pennoyer Architects
Interior Design Director: Alice Engel
Interior Design Associates: Kate McElhiney,
    Madeline Nastala, Cara Wasserman, Lily Wick

HOUSE IN MAINE

Vinalhaven, Maine / 2021
Interior Design: Peter Pennoyer Architects
Interior Design Director: Alice Engel
Interior Design Associates: Kate McElhiney and
    Madeline Nastala

APARTMENT ON EAST 90TH STREET

New York, New York / 2022
Interior Design: Peter Pennoyer Architects
Interior Design Director: Alice Engel
Interior Design Associates: Rebecca Jones and India Dial

KIPS BAY DESIGNER SHOWHOUSE 2022

Palm Beach, Florida / 2022
Interior Design: Peter Pennoyer Architects
Interior Design Director: Alice Engel
Interior Design Associates: India Dial,
    Madeline Nastala, Callie Nelson

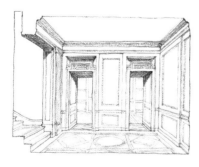

FIFTH AVENUE DUPLEX

New York, New York / 2022
Partner-in-Charge: Jennifer Gerakaris
Design: Eero Schultz
Project Manager: Melissa Voorhees
Associates: Colin Slaten, Marshall Knutson, Thomas
    Lamontagne, Crystal Hanley, Henry Hofmann,
    Emmitt Moore, Philip Davis, John Gibbons
Interior Design: Michael S. Smith Inc.

FIFTH AVENUE APARTMENT

New York, New York / 2022
Partner-in-Charge: Thomas P. R. Nugent
Design: Peter Pennoyer
Project Manager: Ying Liu
Associates: John Gibbons, Steven Aldridge,
    Hayley Fazio
Interior Design: Venfield Inc.

FIFTH AVENUE APARTMENT

New York, New York / 2022
Partner-in-Charge: Thomas P. R. Nugent
Design: Ryan Hughes
Project Manager: Kristen Horigan
Associate: John Gibbons
Interior Design: Stewart Manger Design

GREENWICH VILLAGE TOWNHOUSE

New York, New York / 2022
Partner-in-Charge: Jennifer Gerakaris
Design: Gregory Gilmartin
Project Manager: Lucas Hafeli
Associates: Anastasios Boubalos, John Gibbons,
    Philip Davis, Steven Aldridge, Karile Nefaite,
    Jacob Lee
Interior Design: Peter Pennoyer Architects
Interior Design Director: Alice Engel
Interior Design Associates: Madeline Nastala,
    Callie Nelson, Kate McElhiney

EAST SIDE APARTMENT

(see pages 48–61)
New York, New York / 2022
Partner-in-Charge: Thomas P. R. Nugent
Design: James Taylor
Project Manager: Nicholas Schroeder
Associates: Melissa Voorhees, John Gibbons,
    Philip Davis, Madison Head, Marshall Knutson,
    Colin Slaten
Interior Design: David Kleinberg
    Design Associates

BERKELEY PLACE TOWNHOUSE

Brooklyn, New York / 2022
Interior Design: Peter Pennoyer Architects
Interior Design Director: Alice Engel
Interior Design Associates: India Dial,
    Madeline Nastala, Kate McElhiney

201 WEST 77TH STREET

New York, New York / 2023
Partner-in-Charge: Peter Pennoyer
Design: Peter Pennoyer
Project Managers: Graham Rice and
    Colin Richardson
Associates: Colin Slaten, Daniel Berkman,
    John Gibbons, Emmitt Moore,
    Steven Worthington, Henry Hofmann,
    Mireya Fabregas
Executive Architect: BKSK Architects

FIFTH AVENUE APARTMENT

FIFTH AVENUE APARTMENT: DRAWING FOR A
CAST-GLASS PANEL

GREENWICH VILLAGE TOWNHOUSE

201 WEST 77TH STREET

CAPTAIN'S HOUSE

CAPTAIN'S HOUSE

Centre Island, New York / 2023
Partners-in-Charge: Jennifer Gerakaris and
    James Taylor
Design: Gregory Gilmartin
Project Managers: Crystal Hanley, Hayley Fazio,
    Jacob Lee
Associates: John Gibbons, Lucas Hafeli, Philip
    Davis, Rowan Sloss, Steven Aldridge, John Calvert,
    Elizabeth Reeves, Jacob Lee
Interior Design: Jayne Design Studio

SPANISH-STYLE HOUSE *(see page 17)*

Palm Beach, Florida / 2023
Partner-in-Charge: Timothy Kelly
Design: Benjamin Salling and Peter Pennoyer
Project Manager: Timothy Kelly
Associates: Cleary Shea, John Gibbons, Rowan Sloss,
    Maria Cohn
Interior Design: Hugh Henry of Mlinaric, Henry &
    Zervudachi
Landscape Design: SMI Landscape Architecture

GUILD HALL

GUILD HALL

East Hampton, New York / In Progress
Partners-in-Charge: Peter Pennoyer and
    Timothy Kelly
Design: Peter Pennoyer
Project Managers: Colin Richardson and
    Graham Rice
Associates: Moataz Bashir, Gregory Gilmartin,
    Suchismita Gangopadhyay, Steven Worthington,
    Colin Slaten

EAST SIDE TOWNHOUSE

New York, New York / In Progress
Partner-in-Charge: Jennifer Gerakaris
Design: Peter Pennoyer and Tom Nye
Project Managers: Kathryn Fowler and
    Melissa Voorhees
Associates: Lucas Hafeli, Anastasios Boubalos,
    John Gibbons, Philip Davis, John Calvert, Ben
    Sessa, Elizabeth Reeves, Tom Lamontagne,
    Michael Lawrence
Interior Design: Michael S. Smith Inc.

APARTMENT ON EAST 73RD STREET

New York, New York / In Progress
Partner-in-Charge: Thomas P. R. Nugent
Design: Benjamin Salling
Project Manager: Thomas Lamontagne
Associates: Crystal Hanley, Colin Slaten,
    Marshall Knutson, Myrat Saryyev, John Gibbons,
    Daniel Berkman
Interior Design: Saraphikit–A Design Collective

CLASSICAL HOUSE

Southampton, New York / In Progress
Partner-in-Charge: Jennifer Gerakaris
Design: Gregory Gilmartin
Project Managers: Kristen Horigan, Steven Aldridge,
    Hayley Fazio
Associates: Crystal Hanley, Lucas Hafeli, Karile Nefaite,
    Colin Slaten, Elizabeth Reeves, John Gibbons,
    Philip Davis, Ben Sessa
Interior Design: David Kleinberg Design Associates
Landscape: Hollander Design Landscape Architects

FIFTH AVENUE APARTMENT

New York, New York / In Progress
Partner-in-Charge: Jennifer Gerakaris
Design: Gregory Gilmartin
Project Managers: Karile Nefaite and Daniel Trumble
Associates: Crystal Hanley, Thomas Lamontagne,
    Marshall Knutson, Colin Slaten, Alex Galante,
    John Gibbons, Philip Davis, Henry Hofmann,
    Limor Farfel, Ryan Hughes
Interior Design: Bunny Williams Inc.

LIMESTONE COUNTRY HOUSE

Connecticut / In Progress
Partner-in-Charge: Thomas P. R. Nugent
Design: Gregory Gilmartin and Timothy Kelly
Project Managers: Colin Richardson and
    Nicholas Schroeder
Associates: Steven Aldridge, Jacob Lee, John Gibbons,
    Maria Cohn, John Calvert, Rowan Sloss,
    Philip Davis
Interior Design: Jayne Design Studio
Landscape: Miranda Brooks Landscape Design

FARM IN UPSTATE NEW YORK

Dutchess County, New York / In Progress
Partners-in-Charge: Peter Pennoyer and
  Timothy Kelly
Design: Eero Schultz
Project Managers: Kristen Horigan and
  Colin Richardson
Associates: Jane Pao, Colin Slaten

HOLLYWOOD REGENCY HOUSE

Dallas, Texas / In Progress
Partner-in-Charge: Jennifer Gerakaris
Design: Peter Pennoyer and Eero Schultz
Project Managers: Hannah Rutherfoord and
  Kathryn Fowler
Associates: Steven Aldridge, Colin Slaten,
  Elizabeth Reeves, Yuening Jiang, Idlir Sema,
  John Gibbons, Philip Davis, Steven Worthington
Interior Design: Avrea and Company
Landscape: DDLA Design

HOUSE IN WESTCHESTER

Rye, New York / In Progress
Partner-in-Charge: Thomas P. R. Nugent
Project Manager: Ying Liu
Associates: Missy Morgan and John Gibbons
Interior Design: Peter Pennoyer Architects
Interior Design Director: Alice Engel
Interior Design Associate: Callie Nelson

PARK AVENUE DUPLEX

New York, New York / In Progress
Partner-in-Charge: Thomas P. R. Nugent
Design: Peter Pennoyer
Project Manager: Ying Liu
Associates: Kristen Horigan, William Barker,
  John Gibbons, Philip Davis
Interior Design: KA Design Group

FEDERAL STYLE HOUSE

Dutchess County, New York / In Progress
Partners-in-Charge: Peter Pennoyer and
  Timothy Kelly
Design: Gregory Gilmartin and Steven Aldridge
Project Manager: Timothy Kelly
Associates: Colin Slaten, Alex Galante, William Barker,
  Idlir Sema, Philip Davis
Interior Design: Aero Studios
Landscape: Hollander Design Landscape Architects

EAST SIDE APARTMENT HOUSE

New York, New York / In Progress
Partners-in-Charge: Peter Pennoyer and
  Timothy Kelly
Design: Gregory Gilmartin and Timothy Kelly
Project Manager: Colin Richardson
Associates: Marshall Knutson, Colin Slaten,
  Anastasios Boubalos, Suchismita Gangopadhyay,
  Alex Galante, Thomas Nye, Jane Pao, Missy Morgan,
  John Gibbons

RESTORATION OF THE NOBLE-HARDEE MANSION FOR RALSTON COLLEGE

Savannah, Georgia / In Progress
Partner-in-Charge: Peter Pennoyer
Design: Timothy Kelly and Peter Pennoyer
Project Manager: Timothy Kelly
Associates: Hannah Rutherfoord, Missy Morgan,
  Idlir Sema, John Gibbons
Associated Architect: Sottile & Sottile

CHARLES PLATT HOUSE RENOVATION

New York, New York / In Progress
Partner-in-Charge: Peter Pennoyer
Design: Gregory Gilmartin
Project Manager: Lucas Hafeli
Associates: Steven Aldridge, Melissa Voorhees,
  Crystal Hanley, Elizabeth Reeves, William Barker,
  John Gibbons, Philip Davis, Limor Farfel

HOUSE IN WESTCHESTER

Westchester, New York / In Progress
Partner-in-Charge: Jennifer Gerakaris
Design: Peter Pennoyer and Timothy Kelly
Project Manager: Hannah Rutherfoord
Associates: Lewis Gleason, Steven Aldridge,
  Colin Slaten, Elizabeth Reeves, Yuening Jiang,
  Jason Young Kim, John Gibbons

FIFTH AVENUE MANSION RESTORATION

New York, New York / In Progress
Partner-in-Charge: Jennifer Gerakaris
Design: Gregory Gilmartin
Associates: Lewis Gleason, Colin Slaten, Marshall
  Knutson, Thomas Lamontagne, Lucas Hafeli

PARTY BARN

Chagrin Valley, Ohio / In Progress
Partner-in-Charge: Thomas P. R. Nugent
Design: Thomas P. R. Nugent
Project Manager: Nicholas Schroeder
Associates: Marshall Knutson, Missy Morgan,
  Idlir Sema

PHOTO AND RENDERING CREDITS

All photographs by Eric Piasecki,
with the exception of the
following:

SIMON UPTON:
back of front endpaper, pp. 170–87

Photo by Dave Burk © Empire
State Development | SOM: p. 15

ADAM KANE MACCHIA: p. 19 right

© WILLIAM WALDRON/OTTO:
pp. 62–69

PETER AARON: pp. 124–29

PETER MAUSS/ESTO:
p. 292 bottom right

PETER PENNOYER:
pp. 293 top left, 300 left

ANTON GLIKIN: pp. 293 top
right, 294 second-from-bottom
left, 296 center left, 303

NICK JOHNSON:
p. 293 bottom right

GENEVIEVE IRWIN GOELET:
pp. 294 top left, 295 bottom right

JONATHAN WALLEN: p. 294 right

PHILIP DAVIS: pp. 295 bottom
right, 296 top left, 298 bottom
left, 299 second-from-bottom
right, 300 bottom right

ROB STEPHENSON: p. 297

BENJAMIN SALLING:
p. 298 top left

COLIN SLATEN AND IDLIR SEMA:
p. 298 second-from-top left

COLIN SLATEN AND TIMOTHY
KELLY: p. 298 third-from-top left
and right

MITA BLAND: p. 299 top left

EERO SCHULTZ: p. 299 bottom
left and second-from-top right

REDUNDANT PIXEL:
p. 299 bottom right

COLIN SLATEN, MOATAZ BASHIR,
AND GRAHAM RICE: p. 300 center

COLIN SLATEN, PHILIP DAVIS,
AND HOLLANDER DESIGN
LANDSCAPE ARCHITECTS:
p. 300 top right

ACKNOWLEDGMENTS

The projects included in this, our second monograph, depended on the talent and dedication of so many in our office. I am grateful for the leadership of my partners—Jennifer Gerakaris, Gregory Gilmartin, Tim Kelly, and Tom Nugent—and to all the team members, from designers to project managers to associates, who are recorded in the credits for each project (see pages 292–301). We are also indebted to many more people who make our work possible. First, our clients and the trust they place in us: each structure requires a significant investment—both financial and emotional. We listen carefully to discern their goals, but it is their faith in our abilities that gives us the freedom to explore design once we start drawing. We have been fortunate to have clients who challenge us with visions and inspirations that enrich our work, and we are especially grateful to those who have agreed to allow us to share their projects in this book.

No project is the creation of one architect. Interior designers, clients, landscape architects, and others all have a voice in our process. Our close collaboration with interior designers, who are also listed in the project credits, is a key part of our success, improving our skills and broadening our creative purview from one project to the next. A shared love of design makes these relationships continually rewarding.

Constructing our designs can be challenging. Each project is a one-off. We pay attention to how to build well, and this goal is informed as much by ever-evolving building science as it is by the wisdom of the contractors and craftsmen with whom we collaborate. We are grateful to many builders, including: Brookes + Hill Custom Builders, Brooks & Henderson Building Co., Bulgin & Associates Inc., Clark Construction, Flower Construction, Hedrick Brothers Construction, Hewes & Company Hobbs, Inc., Leeding Builders Group, Lico Contracting Inc., Ryder Construction Inc., Skanska USA Building, SMI Construction Management Inc., Sweeney & Conroy Inc., The Lagasse Group LLC, Uberto, Woolems Inc., Wright & Co Construction Inc., and Zen Restoration Inc.

We also enlist artisans and craftsmen whose special skills refine the character of each project. These artisans include Armadillo Metalworks Inc., Atelier Mériguet-Carrère, Atelier Premiere, Atelier Viollet, Boyd Reath, Budd Woodwork Inc., Cassidy Bros. Forge Inc., E.R.Butler & Co., Féau Boiseries, Foster Reeve, Fresco Decorative Arts, Gregory Muller Associates, Griffin Masonry, Herrick & White, Hyde Park Mouldings, Jamb, Jaroff Studio, Jewett Farms + Co., La Forge De Style, LMC-HB Corp., Louis Beltran Passarelli, Lowe Hardware (Rockland, Maine), Mack Custom Millworking LLC, Miriam Ellner,

Mosaic House, Nancy Lorenz, Orsoni, Pierre Finkelstein, Precision Stone, Remains Lighting Company, Rinck, The Nanz Company, Steven Cavallo, Traditional Cut Stone Ltd., and Turquoise Mountain.

We are fortunate to have continuity in our firm, and the team that made this book is no exception: Anne Walker, my long-time co-author and friend, continued her insightful writing; Lucinda May brought her unerring sense of visual composition; and Yuening Jiang devised a method of using our computer graphics to bring plans to life. Katy Cool, with her writer's eye, polished our text. Sarah Burningham continued to guide our approach, and Elizabeth Keyser organized our efforts to keep us on track. Eric Piasecki, our principal photographer, working with stylist Anne Foxley, created exceptional views. We also benefited from other notable photographers, including Peter Aaron, William Waldron, and Simon Upton.

Finally, the exacting standards of our publisher, Mark Magowan of Vendome Press, led us and his team to make this book the best it could be. Vendome, which has published three of our books, treats each one as an opportunity to excel. Celia Fuller's design eye perfectly framed our projects; the ever-patient Jim Spivey, who oversees production, herded the cats with aplomb; and, lastly, Jackie Decter, our energetic and insightful editor, showed that she cares about every word.

PETER PENNOYER

Peter Pennoyer Architects: City | Country
First published in 2023 by The Vendome Press
Vendome is a registered trademark of The Vendome Press LLC

VENDOME PRESS US
P.O. Box 566
Palm Beach, FL 33480

VENDOME PRESS UK
Worlds End Studio
132–134 Lots Road
London, SW10 0RJ

www.vendomepress.com

Distributed in North America by Abrams Books
Distributed in the United Kingdom, and the rest of the world,
by Thames & Hudson

ISBN 978-0-86565-414-3

PUBLISHERS: Beatrice Vincenzini, Mark Magowan,
   and Francesco Venturi
EDITOR: Jacqueline Decter
PRODUCTION DIRECTOR: Jim Spivey
DESIGNER: Celia Fuller

FLOOR PLANS AND SITE PLANS: Yuening Jiang

Library of Congress Cataloging-in-Publication Data
available upon request

Printed and bound in China by 1010 Printing International Ltd.

FIRST PRINTING

FRONT ENDPAPER
A rendering by Anton Glikin
illustrates the garden façade
of the Arts and Crafts House
in Ohio.

BACK OF FRONT ENDPAPER
A chinoiserie wallpaper
by de Gournay lines the
dressing room in the North
Shore Estate.

PAGE 1
A pencil drawing by Anton
Glikin of a stone tortoise
fountain designed for a new
house in Massachusetts.

PAGES 2–3
At Isola Bella, the dark-
stained shingled house blends
with the conifers of the island.
A grass cart path leads to the
entrance of the house.

PAGES 4–5
In the New Jersey
countryside, PPA designed a
stone house in keeping with
the golden era of country
estates at the turn of the
twentieth century.

PAGES 6–7
At 151 East 78th Street, the
two-story Indiana limestone
base, ornamented with
carved Greek-key panels
and a scrolling pediment and
keystone above the front
doors, connects it to the
residential scale of the street.

PAGE 8
The mahogany woodwork
and colorful patterns of the
wallpaper and rugs give the
interiors of Two Townhouses
into One a vibrant quality.

PAGE 9
A groin-vaulted vestibule
connects the entry hall and
stair hall in the Arts and
Crafts House in Ohio.

PAGE 10
In Two Townhouses into One,
stone steps connect the main
entrance rotunda and the
smaller family entrance.

PAGE 11
The floor in the entrance
rotunda of Two Townhouses
into One is laid in a radiating
pattern of Pietra Serena and
Calacatta Gold marble.

PAGES 20–21
A detail of the carved
American walnut ceiling
in the living room of Two
Townhouses into One,
inspired by ceilings in the
Palazzo Farnese, Rome.

PAGES 138–39
The New Jersey Estate
includes a walled garden that
ties a group of outbuildings to
the main stone house.

THIS PAGE
A design for a grille in the
diplomatic reception room
of the Beaux-Arts Estate in
Dalian, China. Rendering by
Anton Glikin.

FRONT OF BACK ENDPAPER
A stylized chair rail wraps the
curved stair hall in the New
Jersey Estate.

BACK ENDPAPER
Large multi-pane windows light
the apartments at the Benson.
Rendering by Coltan Severson.